Managing Nu1

Managing Nursing Work

Edited by
Barbara Vaughan MSc RGN DipN RNT
and
Moira Pillmoor BSc (Hons) RGN PGCertED RNT RM
With contributions from
Mary FitzGerald RGN DipN CertEd
Jan Snowball BA RGN RCNT RNT
Linda Whitehead RMN

Scutari Press
London

A division of Scutari Projects, the publishing
company of the Royal College of Nursing

First published 1989
Reprinted 1992

British Library Cataloguing in Publication Data

Managing nursing work.
  1. Medicine.   Nursing.   Management
  I. Vaughan, Barbara   II. Pillmoor, Moira
  610.73'068

ISBN 1 871364 09 4

Typeset by Photo·graphics
Printed and bound in Great Britain by
Biddles Ltd, Guildford and King's Lynn

Contents

Preface

The thoughts behind many parts of this book have grown through our contacts with colleagues in both practice and education over the past five years. In particular, the access we have both been given to clinical units to participate in their developments has been of great value. As a result, many of the ideas which are presented have arisen out of our personal experiences.

Our purpose in writing the book is to share some of our conclusions which have arisen from these experiences. It is not our intention to delve deeply into some of the theoretical aspects of the subjects covered, although broad principles have been included and recommendations are given for further reading. Rather, we hope to present a practical guide which may act as an introduction to the complex world of managing nursing work and hope that it will be of use to others.

Barbara Vaughan
Moira Pillmoor
1988

Acknowledgements

This book is the product not only of the writers' perseverance and determination but also of those who have provided support and encouragement throughout: they are too numerous to mention individually but will know themselves. Without them it could not have been done.

Special thanks to John for his unstinting devotion, above the call of duty!

BV
MP

Introduction

As nurses we are all aware of the changes which are taking place around us at a fairly rapid pace. In principle, most of us accept these changes with resigned, and even cheerful, optimism. However, there are times when difficulties may arise in trying to identify what is happening and then to alter work practices accordingly. Indeed, there are some who will overtly oppose change at all costs since the reasoning behind it is not always clear and the outcomes are ill defined.

This book is intended to introduce nurses to some of the underlying factors which are currently influencing nursing and to identify ways in which these may affect practice. Much of the information that is required for effective clinical management can be found throughout the literature but it is difficult to find and collate – it has been brought together here for ease of access, particularly in relation to work organisation and the skills required for effective practice. Some practical ideas on how to respond to the demands of nursing have been included, and we hope that these will be of use.

This book should also be seen as a foundation on which further work can be built rather than as the 'ultimate text' to be used in isolation. It is in two sections, which deal respectively with the underlying reasons for change and some of the related skills that are necessary for success.

Firstly, it is necessary to identify some of the issues surrounding the plethora of changes which have been taking place in recent years. All too frequently, these have become confused and even lost their meaning in the frantic rush to meet demands. This rush has also led, in some instances, to inaccurate interpretation of the way in which nursing practice may be developed, and resultant difficulties have led to frustration and feelings of guilt and hopelessness on the part of the practitioner.

It is the purpose here to reintroduce some of the most significant changes which have occurred in the arena of nursing in recent years and identify the implications for nursing with particular reference to the management and organisation of work.

Secondly, it is now recognised that there are many factors which can influence the delivery of the nursing service beyond direct patient care. Some of these factors, such as the way in which nursing work is managed and the importance of job satisfaction for staff, will be raised in Part I. In Part II, a more detailed look is taken at the ways in which we can help to create an environment which will facilitate good nursing. Taking care of ourselves and the people we work with are essential prerequisites if we wish to get the best out of staff. Ensuring that people feel secure and valued in their work, and know what is expected of them and how well they are performing, all lead to a productive work-team. Managing time, setting priorities and understanding the dilemmas we often face in our day-to-day work can ease the pressure under which we all function.

There are so many factors which can influence how nursing work is facilitated that a tome would be necessary to cover them all. However, some of the key issues that we consider important have been included in Part II of this book. Each subject is dealt with separately although, in reality, all are closely interrelated. An indication of the content of each chapter is given at the beginning, followed by an introduction to the subject under discussion and some hints or guides as to how they apply to practice. At the end of each chapter there is a short guide to further reading, since we do not intend to do more than offer a starting point from which you may begin to explore further. The exercises are by no means compulsory but may help in making the points which we raise more explicit.

Part I

1
Developing Trends in Nursing

INTRODUCTION

In today's society there is a strong emphasis on the need for us all to re-examine the manner in which we do things and to question whether there are better, more efficient ways of undertaking our work. Nurses, like everyone else, are reviewing some of the traditional practices which have been adhered to for so long and asking whether they are still appropriate. Such things as the nursing process, models for practice and primary nursing are frequently referred to in the journals. The implication of such discussions is that change is in the air, and not least amongst the changes is the need to review the way in which nursing work is managed. Very broadly, the purpose of a manager is to 'get work out of people'. We can no longer afford to be inefficient about the way we use the precious resources available to us. Similarly, we need to find ways of retaining people's motivation and enthusiasm for their work in order that they are happy and fulfilled, so give of their best.

WHY CHANGE?

Change is a normal part of our everyday lives. We are perpetually responding to all the things that go on around us, taking note of new ideas and responding to new information by adjusting our behaviour according to the circumstances in which we find ourselves. Sometimes, the changes occur suddenly in response to a dramatic life event such as a new job, a different relationship or an unexpected illness. At other times, the changes occur very slowly as the things that affect us creep up almost unnoticed. Some people are hardly aware of the increasing years or the shift in emphasis of the views of society on such major issues as the sanctity of life, sexuality or human rights.

Just as an individual changes over a period of time, so does the place in society taken by some service-orientated occupations. Looking back over the past century, several alterations can be seen to have occurred in nursing, influenced not only by nurses themselves but also by all the other events that are going on in society at large. Obvious factors are such things as the changing role of women, particularly in an occupation which is still predominantly female. Similarly, increases in the technology and management of disease have had a significant impact on nursing. Bevis (1978) describes a definite shift in the 1950s to what she calls the 'pragmatic' nurse, one who responded rapidly to the technological growth which was occurring at that time, with a corresponding 'extension' of the nurse's role to include many new technical tasks. The setting up in the 1970s of the then Joint Board of Clinical Nursing Studies, offering nurses an opportunity to develop some of the skills required to cope with this change, is an example of how nurses responded. An examination of the curricula for those early courses demonstrates that at that time the emphasis was still on the management of disease, or health-care problems after they had occurred, with only a small amount of time devoted to other aspects of health care such as teaching or prevention.

Another change in society, which is occurring in the late eighties and may be more important to us as nurses, is the value that people now place on managing their own health. There is a gradual shift away from a reliance on health-care workers to control and manage all aspects of the service towards a right of people to have some say in the management of their own health. The establishment of such groups as the National Childbirth Trust and the College of Health exemplifies such a move. People are starting to question whether technology alone is a sufficient answer to their health needs. In no way does this lessen the importance of new technology. What it does mean is that we, as nurses, must review the service that we offer the public, and actively plan ways in which we can develop in order to meet their newly-recognised needs.

ILLNESS AND HEALTH

One of the most important shifts that has happened in the past few years is the movement away from a disease-centred service, aimed at managing illness or controlling the symptoms once they have occurred, towards a service aimed at preventing disease and promoting health. Thus, there is a change of emphasis towards the prevention of ill health rather than its cure. Pietroni (1986) has likened our so-called 'health service' to a mechanic mending a fault without discovering why it has occurred in the first place. A single symptom or disease process is isolated and treated without investigating the multiplicity of underlying factors which could all have played their part in causing the presenting difficulties. For example, regardless of the knowledge of the relationship between stress and hypertension and the effectiveness of using relaxation as a method of managing this condition (Schwartz, 1975), there are only a very few centres which go beyond the use of drug therapy to control blood pressure. Often only superficial advice about 'relaxing more' is given without any guidance on how this may be achieved. Yet if our goal is to promote health, curing or controlling disease is not sufficient. Instead, we must start seeking information about why ill health occurs and start sharing that information with the people who seek help. In this way we can help them to manage their own lives in such a way as to maintain or achieve a state which they see as healthy.

Such a shift has obvious implications for nurses. A large proportion of nursing time has been spent traditionally in providing a service for people who are already ill (diseased), through fulfilment of medical orders – treatment of the disease and 'doing' things for people while they are incapacitated. If the service which nurses offer is viewed from a health rather than an illness stance then changes must take place in that service. Neuman (1982) very clearly outlines three areas of nursing function which reflect such a change. She describes them as:

'Primary intervention . . . where actions are taken to avoid health difficulties occurring, such as teaching people ways of keeping fit.'

'Secondary interventions . . . where actions are taken to help people to return to a level of health which they find acceptable or to adapt in such a way that they can cope with their new level of health.'

'Tertiary intervention . . . where steps are taken to ensure that an agreed "level of wellness" is maintained.'

Such a view is clearly different from our more traditional approach of mending a fault once it has occurred without investigating how it could have been prevented or can be avoided in the future. Furthermore, it offers a wide opportunity for nurses to expand their contribution to health care.

FROM ROUTINISATION TO DELIBERATE ACTION

If the service we offer changes, there are several underlying things which will have to be reviewed. Firstly, there are clear implications for reconsidering the knowledge base from which we practise.

Secondly, new skills must be learnt, particularly in the field of teaching and health promotion. Thirdly, we must seek alternative ways of managing and organising the work we undertake in order to facilitate such an approach.

If we recognise that there will always be a multiplicity of causes which can all contribute to any given situation, then we must develop our skills of assessment in order to plan nursing effectively. Similarly, we cannot expect to follow fixed procedures which relate to a named disease or illness since it is unlikely that two people will have the same combination of contributing factors and, consequently, their individual needs for nursing may well be different, as will be the care that they require.

Since many of the underlying causes which have contributed to the onset of a disease are social or psychological in origin, an understanding of both sociology and psychology becomes essential for nurses. It is only with such understanding that we can begin to widen the base from which we practise. The movement which is occurring in views of health and illness is shown in Figure 1.1. It is by no means complete and there are still many people who view illness from a purely physiological stance. Yet, if we wish to be in a position to help those clients or patients who take a wider view we also must develop our services.

The time has gone when we could rely on the routine procedures which have served us for so long. We have to move from our traditional approach of following set patterns and routinising the care we offer to an approach based on conscious decision-making, taking into account the individual needs of each patient alongside the needs of others who require our services. We have to learn principles which can be adapted in such a way that we can respond to the different situations of people and make plans which suit them personally. If we value this approach to nursing, we

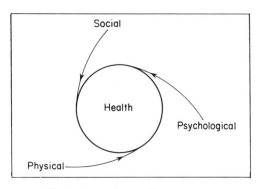

Fig 1.1 Factors affecting health

must also look at the way in which we work. We can no longer expect to be able to provide a service for patients within our traditional ways of managing nursing work. Instead, we must consider how we can develop methods which are better suited to current needs and which allow sufficient flexibility for both patients and nurses to demonstrate their individual strengths, and thus to grow.

POWER IN HEALTH CARE

Many people view power in a negative manner, seeing it as something that is undesirable. Yet, the wise use of power can be a very positive influence (Figure 1.2). Claus and Bailey (1977) present such a positive model of power, suggesting that there are three underlying factors, namely:

- the strength . . . that is an awareness of one's own ability and skills
- the energy . . . that is the will to act and a positive use of the energy
- the action . . . the powerful person will actually act in order to solve problems and make decisions

Fig 1.2 Power can be positive

Power can be claimed from a number of different sources. Firstly, it can be based on an individual's position within an organisation. In this situation it is 'given' through a formal acknowledgement of authority in certain circumstances. Alternatively, power can be gained through personal growth and development in such a way as to allow the individual concerned the strength to influence others. Finally, power can be socially based through groups acting in a cohesive manner and uniting to gain strength.

The society we live in has not only accepted but also encouraged a situation in health care where all the power, and therefore control of resources, has been vested in a single discipline, namely medicine. While other disciplines may have been encouraged by doctors to take on some of their delegated tasks, the boundaries of their authority have also been strictly controlled. One outcome of this situation has been the stunting of potential of other disciplines which contribute to the overall service, so that, instead of each occupational group developing its unique contribution, they have all grown in such a way as to support medicine. Nowhere can this be seen more vividly than in nursing, where an emphasis has been placed on extending the nursing function to take on board new tasks which are derived from a disease-centred approach, rather than expanding the role towards deepening our understanding of ways in which the nursing function can support the promotion of health.

It is only in recent years that nurses have begun to recognise the potential importance of their autonomous function within health care which is independent of, but complementary to, other health-care workers within the service as a whole. Autonomy does not imply that one occupational group can act without consideration for others, rather that, within a defined area, the practitioners concerned can control and manage their own work, taking into account the contribution of other services and the needs of the organisation as a whole. This will inevitably place some constraints on the degree of freedom of each occupational group but is nevertheless essential in order to contribute to the total service.

It is, however, undesirable to argue for the recognition of autonomy in nursing unless nursing actions move from a reactive approach, largely based on tradition, routine and medical direction, to a situation of deliberate decision-making. We must progress to a position where actions are founded on knowledge, are defensible and are directed towards the achievement of a previously defined goal. Without such conditions, a move towards autonomous practice in nursing would be both undesirable and dangerous.

Another constraint on the growth of nursing has been the rigid bureaucratic structure which has been dominant for so long. The plethora of rigid rules, regulations, procedures and practice, with a clearly-defined hierarchy seen within our hospitals, is, in itself, antithetical to growth. If we wish to allow individuals in our discipline to develop to their full potential, we must also allow them room to do so; this will inevitably require an alteration in the structuring of the nursing service.

It is not only the rigid hierarchical structure which has, in the past, inhibited potential development in nursing, but also the organisational structure within which it works. In any area where resources are short it is likely that a monopoly will lie with the most powerful group. In the past it has been medicine that has held the key to all resources, acting as gatekeeper, regardless of the expertise of other groups: thus, there has been no direct access for the public to any health-care worker without first passing through the medical portal. So referral to the physiotherapist for help with muscular pain, to the occupational therapist for advice about kitchen aids or to nurses for assistance in managing activities of daily living, has all been made through medicine (Figure 1.3).

Fig 1.3   The gatekeeper of all resources

It may be that the time has come to question such a situation and ask whether or not it is entirely appropriate. Long waiting times can occur because of the heavy pressure placed on outpatient departments, with the resultant delay in access to the appropriate health-care worker: indeed; there is now some evidence to suggest that in some circumstances people would prefer to seek advice initially from nurses (Stilwell, 1982). Not only would this meet a recognised need in society but it would also relieve some of the pressure from doctors and allow them more time to attend to those whose primary need is for medical help.

In reality, the group with the greatest power is likely to make the greatest impact when competing for resources. The imbalance which can occur as a result is not always in the interest of the total service. For example, rapid advances in science and technology have resulted in more people being able to receive the technical treatment they require more quickly; however, the cost of an increase in this aspect of care has often been met by reductions in funding to other areas, such as nursing, so making it difficult to respond to the corresponding increase in workload. Through such circumstances, their contribution to care may suffer as, indeed, may the services offered to those requiring less technical care, such as the elderly.

It is power, based on knowledge of the effects of nursing action, which could potentially rebalance this situation, enabling nurses to stand alongside other occupational groups in health care and contribute on an equal footing. Knowledge-based power is not only effective in maintaining partnership and equality within the health-care team but can also act as a positive force in developing partnership relationships with clients or consumers. Over the past two decades there has been a steadily growing increase in people's awareness of their own health and their right to have some control over how it is managed. Indeed, there has been a dramatic increase in people's understanding and knowledge about health and an increasing interest in the different ways in which a problem can be handled. Many people are no longer satisfied with the role of the passive recipient of treatment, taking their medicine as directed without knowing why. Surely such a change in society can only be good? It is certainly exemplified by the growing number of specialised lay groups who have a wealth of understanding about their own area of interest.

Such a change has significant implications for nursing practice. It is no longer acceptable for any health-care worker, including the nurse, to direct a patient to follow a given course of action and expect compliance without explanation. Not only must we be able to give a sound rationale for recommending a course of action but we must also be prepared to take into account the personal preferences, experience and knowledge of the person to whom the service is offered. It may be that some people want firm direction, particularly if they are feeling very unwell. However, there is an equal chance that they may prefer to participate actively in the decisions which are made about their own treatment. There is ample evidence that the degree of compliance with directions from health-care workers is poor but that involvement, shared planning and choice will, with flexibility to suit individual needs, increase the compliance. Recognition of this factor has significant economic implications as well as being of benefit to the people concerned.

If such views are taken as being both important and desirable, the reality of a need to review our current practice must be faced. Firstly, the body of knowledge on which practice is based must be sound, up to date and continually growing. Secondly, the relationship between the nurse and the patient must move from one of directorship to one of partnership. Thirdly, the organisational structure in which nursing works must be transformed to move from a tight hierarchy to a structure which fosters growth.

THE GROWTH OF PROFESSIONALISM

For many years now, an argument has raged about whether or not nursing is a profession. It has been suggested that, in the precise sociological meaning of the word, nursing will never gain professional status, since it will always be dependent on medicine (Goode, 1969). Indeed, it can be argued that there are some characteristics of professional status which would be undesirable in today's society. In particular, the monopoly of control over resources and knowledge is questionable, since many of the developments within health care are dependent on sharing these things.

Yet there are some characteristics of professional behaviour which are desirable in any occupational group offering a service to the public. These include such things as a continued pattern of learning and updating of knowledge, as well as a willingness to accept responsibility and to stand accountable for one's own practice (Figure 1.4).

In order to contribute to a service which is orientated towards health, based on rational decision-making and where the autonomous function of nursing is recognised and acknowledged, all nurses must recognise their own responsibilities. Maintaining knowledge of current developments in practice is no longer an optional extra but an essential requirement. From a professional perspective, following rules will no longer be an acceptable excuse for poor practice if the outcome is not suitable for individual clients' needs. Vicarious responsibility for the practising nurse, that is responsibility held by the health authority on the nurse's behalf, will not cover outmoded practice, nor should it. The implications for nurses are obvious. Not only must they examine the basis from which they practise but also the structure in which such a service is offered.

Fig 1.4 The professional practitioner

MODELS FOR PRACTICE

The growing concern for a need to clarify exactly what nursing practice is has led to many people outlining 'models of nursing', or sets of interrelated ideas which, when linked together, adequately describe nursing. Essentially, a conceptual model will view all the concepts or ideas which the author sees as relevant to nursing and comment on each one, describing its relationship to practice (Pearson and Vaughan, 1986). There are some common views in most of the models which reflect the changing opinions which have occurred in recent times. The changes have not been revolutionary in nature – rather, they have happened gradually, and in some cases the significance for nursing practice has been slow to be noticed. Thus, different people will be at different stages on a continuum of development. Figure 1.5 summarises some of the changes which have occurred and shows the implications for practice.

If such changes are desirable in nursing practice, we must look seriously at all these issues and make careful plans for the future. It is with these points in mind that this book has been prepared in an attempt to introduce some of the basic principles behind organising nursing work. We hope it is 'people-centred', clarifying some of the terms that are commonly used and offering an introduction to some of the skills associated with the management components of our work. It is seen as an introductory text, highlighting the issues which require consideration, giving some introductory material and guiding towards further investigation.

Concept	From	To	Implications
People	Seen as biological creatures subject to disease	Viewed holistically with a right to contribute to the management of their own health	Changes in knowledge base and criteria for assessment
Health	The absence of disease	A feeling of well-being	People's own feelings and wishes about their own health must be taken into account
Goals of practice	Cure above all else	Achievement of maximum independence, etc.	Negotiation with each person to identify personal wishes
Relationships	Directive approach with expectation of compliance	Shared decision-making	New skills in interpersonal relationships
Method	Routinised approach to nursing	A systematic approach to nursing	Development of sound knowledge base for practice
Organisation	A rigid bureaucratic system	A professional model of practice	Changes in methods of organising work and modes of practice

Fig 1.5 Changes in practice

2
Implications for Practice

An evolving service with a shift of focus from disease and illness to individuals and their health must create far-reaching implications for all those who have responsibility for the provision and maintenance of that service. Nursing is one of the many facets of health care and the nurse is an independent but integrated member of the health-care team; therefore, nurses, as health workers, must take stock and assess and identify the implications that this change has for their special discipline. Areas or aspects of nursing which require examination include:

- Conceptualisation of nursing and the adoption of clearly-identified models for clinical practice, research and education (a philosophy of care)
- Quality assurance
- Professional education
- Relationships with clients and colleagues
- Accountability and responsibility
- Formal structure and organisation of nursing

A PHILOSOPHY OF CARE

The ability to conceptualise implies the mental capacity to visualise a subject and identify or classify all its components. Thus, conceptualisation is an essential prerequisite within any discipline, including nursing, in order to clarify its purpose and give it direction. However, it must be an ongoing and dynamic process if the discipline hopes to meet the continually changing needs of the society it serves. A philosophy of nursing, or model, will help nurses to identify ideas and issues to which they should address themselves, and elaborate on them according to the particular perspective that has been taken (see Chapter 6).

Currently, the view is held by many nurse theorists that there are four clearly identifiable concepts which are central to the discussion of nursing (Bush, 1979; Fawcett, 1978). Three of these concepts can be thought of as relating to the 'ingredients' of nursing, and the fourth to the 'method or activities' of nursing known as the nursing process. Thus, the aims of nursing are derived from the values expressed in the 'ingredients' and the activities are the means by which these aims are achieved.

Ingredients of Nursing

The ingredients of nursing are the basic building-blocks and must relate to the change in focus from disease and illness to people as individuals and their health (Figure 2.1). The three main components which relate to the aims of nursing are:

1. The person or people receiving nursing
2. The environment in which the person lives and, if different, the environment where nursing is to be delivered
3. The health status of the person or people

Fig 2.1 The recipe for success

It is worth noting here that this 'process of nursing' is not, in itself, a guarantee of a personalised service. It is only a method, albeit a method which can lend itself to such an aim. However, its success is dependent on the exposition of the ideas and values contained in the concepts relating to the 'ingredients' of nursing.

For a framework to give direction, clear statements must be made about the beliefs and values relating to these main ingredients. From a review of published work (Nightingale, 1859;

Roy, 1976; Orem, 1980; King, 1981; Roper et al, 1985) it can be seen that the beliefs and values vary according to the writers' analysis and evaluation of the three components. In some instances these variations are fundamental in nature, but others are a product of language and expression; for example, while nearly all authors recognise holism as a common concept, some derive their thinking from developmental theory and others from symbolic interaction.

The Nursing Process: Method or Activities of Nursing

As the ingredients of nursing must relate to the needs and demands of present-day society, so must the method or activities of nursing. Society is demanding explanation and individual accountability for all actions. Decision-making must increasingly have its roots firmly embedded in a systematic base, rather than one of custom and practice or routine. Many nurses believe that they have always used a systematic or scientific approach to care, but there is considerable evidence which says that much nursing work is still embedded in tradition rather than being planned purposefully, and it is deliberate action which is desired.

Many nurses agree that the activities of nursing should be based on a systematic approach which relates to the action research model. This scientific way of thinking is now well recognised and known as the nursing process. Such an approach can, however, be applied to any organised procedure and is not exclusive to nursing.

'Activities' implies what nurses do. 'Systematic' and 'scientific' imply ordered and deliberate activity based on knowledge. The activities enable nurses to meet needs, solve problems and answer questions relating to health care within the bounds of their discipline.

The activities of nursing can be broken down into a series of steps or stages. For the purpose of explanation, seven are described here separately although, in reality, they often overlap.

1. Data Collection

Information is collected according to the ideas and values contained within the four concepts identified earlier, namely, people, their environment, the environment where care is given, and their health status. The way in which each of these ingredients is considered will identify which information is important and should be collected. It will also determine attitudes and behaviours to be adopted during the process of data collection. Personalisation is achieved by collecting only that data which is relevant to a given individual in a given situation and which he or she wishes to reveal. The term *appropriate* is the key word in data collection and has implications for both clinicians and general managers. As a general guide, collect:

- Only appropriate data (guided by the conceptual framework)
- At an appropriate time
- In an appropriate place (curtains are not soundproof!)
- By an appropriate method, and
- By an appropriate person (able to discriminate between relevant and irrelevant information)

2. *Analysis of Data*

Data is analysed by comparing and contrasting findings against the ideas and values stated in the four main concepts, but incorporating the patient's own views. This will include comparisons with known physical, psychological and social norms, taking into account individual variations. The purpose of the analysis is to reveal any health-care needs, problems or questions. It must be borne in mind, however, that not all people view their own health in the same way and a situation which may seem problematic or questionable to one person may be quite acceptable to another.

Identification of a problem or problems would permit the use of the term 'problem-solving' in relation to this systematic approach to nursing. Some people view 'problems' in a negative light. Yet, if they are considered simply as unmet needs, this negative connotation is lost and their clarification can give a positive focus to the planning of care.

3. *Objectives or Goals of Nursing*

Objectives or goals are statements of desired outcomes which may be sought by the person receiving nursing care. These statements may be both 'quantitative', using specific measurements such as temperature or weight, and 'qualitative', using less rigid criteria, in nature and will relate to the needs, problems or questions identified on analysis. Once identified, they need to be set in an order of priority that is agreeable both to the client and the nurse. There may be times when a life-threatening condition, such as severe respiratory distress, will outweigh all other needs and must be attended to first of all; at other times, priorities may have to be negotiated.

4. Review and Choose

Activity Four involves a review of the possible therapeutic actions which may help to achieve the desired outcome. Obviously, this requires considerable knowledge on the part of the nurse since he or she must be conversant with a whole range of approaches which could be helpful. The application of a routine solution to a routine problem is no longer acceptable. This is not to deny the presence of 'usual' problems for many patients in the same situation; rather, it means that the manner in which the problem is handled is specific to the particular person concerned.

5. Prescription

Activity Five is the selection of the therapeutic actions to be tried. As there is usually more than one way tc achieve a desired outcome, careful consideration of all possible options is required (Figure 2.2). Analysis and evaluation of each option is influenced by:

- Knowledge derived from research
- The law
- Morality and ethics
- Technology available
- Resources
- Common sense
- Professional judgment
- Intuition
- Local policy

It is desirable that the therapeutic action chosen is selected on the basis of knowledge derived from research. Undoubtedly, it is also necessary to select on the basis of the less rigid and strict domain of human experience which includes common sense and intuition. However, even our intuitive responses are founded on more than a gut reaction – they are steeped in a wealth of past experience and insight into the effectiveness of nursing actions.

All selected actions, whatever their origins, should be submitted to deliberate observation in order to facilitate evaluation of them in relation to the specific setting in which they have been used. Such findings can then be incorporated into the body of knowledge from which future care is planned. It is only through this approach that we can begin to understand some of the complex decisions that many nurses make which are often put down to 'instinct' or 'gut reaction' but which, in reality, are a very skilled interpretation of all the presenting information (Schon, 1984).

Fig 2.2 There's more than one way . . .

6. *Implementation of Action*

All therapeutic actions are carried out in such a way as to uphold the views contained in the chosen framework. Provided that there is agreement about the framework, the attitudes and behaviours of the practitioners are also directed by the same underlying beliefs and values. The actions themselves should be deliberately observed throughout the whole process in order to be able to judge their usefulness.

7. *Analysis and Evaluation*

The observations made during the implementation stage are examined for their effectiveness in both qualitative and quantitative terms. The effect, or actual outcome, is then compared with the desired outcome in order to establish whether the objectives or stated goals have been achieved.

Much criticism has been levied at this approach or method of delivering care. However, if nurses are to become independent and autonomous practitioners, we must adopt a method which will withstand the questioning and scrutiny of the consumer and will facilitate communication with other health-care workers. Without the information which becomes available to us through such an approach, it is impossible to answer for our actions either to colleagues or clients. Reliance on routine and tradition alone does not permit us to account in a rational and systematic way for the work which we undertake, and negates our position within the health-care team. This method will also facilitate the setting of standards, since valid information becomes available about the care which has been given and its effect. Such information is also essential when considering quality assurance. Lastly but not least, using a method of this kind helps to ensure the continuing development of nursing knowledge.

QUALITY ASSURANCE

Quality assurance is an activity which has, in recent years, become relevant, not just to the health service, but to all other industries and organisations. Society seeks assurance that the services being offered meet certain criteria and standards, and these standards of performance are determined both by the consumer of the service and by the professional or occupational group providing the service. The nurse, as a member of the health-care team, is responsible and accountable for the quality of the nursing service offered to the client or consumer. The quality of nursing is part of, and therefore reflected in, the overall evaluation.

Some work practices and other factors which play a part in assuring the quality of the nursing service are as follows.

1. Nurses must be able to identify, understand and implement their specific contribution as members of the health-care team. A clear conceptual picture of nursing will help nurses to identify the roles they can take through clarification of those ideas, values and issues to which nurses should be addressing themselves.

2. Identification and adoption of a conceptual framework on which practice is based facilitates the setting of standards. Evaluation of outcomes, both qualitatively and quantitatively, in relationship to those standards is then possible. This is achieved through identification of the 'ingredients' of nursing and the use of a systematic approach to the delivery of care.

3. A description of work to be done helps to define work parameters within the discipline of nursing and makes it possible to assign responsibility for that work to appropriate workers. The description arises, again, from the conceptual framework, which clearly states the activities of nursing.

4. Selection of the people to do the job, matching the work with each nurse practitioner's expertise, capabilities and experience.

5. Performance review, which monitors performance in the job and directs programmes of development to meet changing needs.

6. The educational process directed by the conceptual framework introduces the student of nursing to the knowledge, skills and attitudes required for the job to be undertaken. Continuing education facilitates the continued growth and development of nurses, which is an essential requirement in order to keep pace with, or even ahead of, demands being made by an ever-changing society.

7. Application of research findings, which ensures a sound knowledge base for clinical decision-making.

8. The appreciation and use of deliberate observation in relationship to all therapeutic actions.

9. Registration and employment of practitioners only on certification of competence.

10. Selection of students who potentially have the ability, capability, personality and motivation to be registered nurse practitioners.

11. Local policies and procedures which relate to health-care rights and standards, and which have the power of enforcement through the contract of employment.

12. Legislation, which relates to health-care rights and standards, and has the power of enforcement through legal channels.

13. Audit/unit appraisal, that is the collecting of data regarding identified quality items, comparison of data against established standards of those items and, finally, the judgment of performance.

14. Monitoring of consumer satisfaction with the service received gives some indication of health-care needs and whether they are being met.

PROFESSIONAL EDUCATION

Education of the student of nursing and the continuing education of the nurse have become major issues of importance over the past fifty years, with reports and enquiries being commissioned by government, the statutory body and the professional organisations (Athlone, 1938; Horder, 1942; Wood, 1947; Platt, 1964; Judge, 1985; UKCC Project 2000, 1986).

Education must meet the needs of students of the future in such a way as to enable them to function as independent practitioners. A great number of nurses still see education as a skills-dominated process, driven by the need to carry out activities which are generated by the organisation or by other groups, such as doctors. However, nurse practitioners will generate their own activities, a process which will require a great deal more than the development of mechanical skills and will also be dependent on the cognitive domain of learning. These activities include the ability to make decisions, as well as the application of therapies such as counselling and teaching.

RELATIONSHIPS

The health service is primarily for people. It can be argued that nurses have always had to relate to people, whether they are colleagues in other disciplines or clients. That may well be so. However, the evolving work system is creating changes which have implications not only for relationships and communication skills within the interdisciplinary team but also between nurses and clients.

Interdisciplinary Relationships: Partnership and the Health-Care Team

One of the concepts most central to the issue of relationships in a team is the notion of all partners playing an equal, participatory role. It is assumed that health care is delivered by teams of professionals, all working together to achieve common objectives. However, this is not always supported by research findings: both Dingwall (1980) and Reedy (1980) question the use of the word 'team' to describe the present work practices of the representative disciplines. Reedy (1980) and Armitage (1983) claim that 'collaboration' is a more appropriate term and that those collaborative groups do not demonstrate equality of partnership or, for that matter, necessarily share the same values or perceived outcomes. If the notion of the team approach is to be valued and pursued in the future, not just nursing but all disciplines must review the concept of teamwork in the light of the professional development of the groups, the subsequent struggle for autonomy which this will bring and the needed shift in power from the already autonomous medical profession (Figure 2.3).

However, to be equal, nurses must learn to value themselves, recognising their worth and the unique contribution they make

Fig 2.3 Teams pull together

to health care. Self-image is all important. It is the driving force behind the discipline and is one of the major factors influencing both the views held by, and the relationship which develops between, nursing and other related disciplines as well as with clients.

Development of an individual practitioner (Stilwell, 1982) who is responsible and accountable for the nursing service, and the subsequent acceptance of nurses in this role by both clients and other disciplines, is something which many are seeking. Some things which may help in a movement in this direction include:

- Clarifying the concept of nursing which will help to identify issues to be addressed and the method by which nursing problems or questions are tackled
- The adoption of a systematic method of practice
- Building up nursing theory by means of research which is identified within the conceptual framework
- Education of students of nursing with the clearly identified practitioner role in view
- Continuing education for the present body of nurses which will facilitate a change to the practitioner role
- Education for other health-care disciplines and clients about the role and function of the nurse

The Nurse and the Client

Partnership with a client can be seen as a contract and implies the active participation of the client in his or her care. It is recognised that, for maximum effectiveness, clients must be included in all steps of the nursing process. However, for partnership to exist, clients must be informed, that is they must be in receipt of information regarding the situation, the possible outcomes and the possible choice of actions which may be taken to achieve those outcomes. Information is a source of legitimate power (Bond and Bond, 1986). Currently, many professional people are still withholding information from clients 'in their best interest', a practice which does not lend itself to partnership. The publication of the Patients' Charters and the Data Protection Act 1986 has highlighted the right of individuals to be in full receipt of information regarding their health status and the care which is available and, even though some medical information can still be withheld, this is a step in the right direction. The nurse practitioner must, therefore, be prepared to give information to clients which will facilitate true partnership and informed agreement in all matters concerning their nursing.

The effect of retaining or withholding information is to deny clients the right of equal status. It also implies that they are considered to be incapable of making a decision about their own lives and health care, which is surely unacceptable.

Communication

The stability, strength and effectiveness of a relationship depend on many factors, but one of the most important is communication. For a therapeutic relationship to exist, there must be open communication between the people involved. It is only in fairly recent times that it has been recognised that people are not inherently good communicators, and that communication skills can, and should, be taught to both students and trained nurses (Faulkner, 1980).

ACCOUNTABILITY AND RESPONSIBILITY

In order to be accountable, it is not sufficient just to accept responsibility for actions – nurses must also be able and willing to justify and explain those actions (Lewis and Batey, 1982). Accountability is not in itself new to nursing in that nurses, both as members of a discipline and as private citizens, have always been accountable for their actions. However, owing to the bureaucratic structure of the health service, it has been possible for individuals to remain 'incognito' and present a faceless front to the public. Bureaucratic organisations are characterised by hierarchy and formal rules and regulations which have made it very difficult to establish individual accountability.

Up to the present time, much nursing work has been generated through the decision-making of other disciplines, mainly medicine, so accountability has only pertained to the carrying out of orders, and not to the decision-making surrounding the orders or instructions. If nurses are to take on a discrete role in the health-care team and use a systematic approach to their own work, they must also recognise their responsibility, and hence accountability, not only for the implementation of the therapeutic actions but also for the decision-making which surrounds them.

The four main lines of accountability are shown in Figure 2.4. Particular note should be taken of the differentiation which exists between accountability to the statutory body (UKCC) and the employer or organisation. Previously this distinction has not been made clear but it is now widely acknowledged that nurses are accountable as individuals and, as such, must answer for their own actions to their professional representatives. Inclusion of clients, as a separate group to whom they must account, emphasises both the rights of that group and the need for nurses to work from a sound knowledge base in a systematic fashion.

The implications of being accountable are that one is answerable to others for one's actions and that, if one is unable to demonstrate that they were reasonable in the circumstances, corrective steps may be taken. These may only take the form of remedial recommendations or can be as extreme as to lead to removal from the professional register. In some instances, monetary payment may be required for damages which have occurred as an outcome of inappropriate behaviour. In the past it has been common practice for the employing authority to accept vicarious responsibility for nurses' actions but this may no longer always be the case.

FORMAL STRUCTURE AND ORGANISATION OF NURSING

The traditional hierarchical structure of nursing reflects the bureaucratic nature of the present health-care system. It could be argued that there are both vertical and horizontal structural lines in nursing. For example, all registered nurses can be placed in a horizontal relationship with one another by virtue of their qualification, but they are employed in different positions in the organisation which are classified vertically. Furthermore, when each of these structures is analysed it can be seen that power of authority and prestige relates only to the vertical structures and, the greater the input is to organisational management, the higher the position is on this line. Thus, there can be power differences

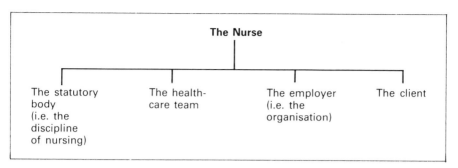

Fig 2.4   Lines of accountability

between those who claim to be in the same work group (Simpson, 1979).

This hierarchical power order in nursing does not facilitate individual accountability, autonomous practice, personalisation of the service and the use of a systematic approach. There is a need for equal power-sharing with each person's contribution to the total service of care delivery being fully recognised. Such a suggestion is covered further in part II of this book but will have obvious implications for such things as salary scales, methods of work, job descriptions and criteria for appointment to posts.

In this chapter, some of the issues which are concerned with our approach to practice have been raised and an outline offered of the related points. Some of these things will be returned to in the second half of this book, looking more specifically at the skills which are needed and ways in which we may achieve them. However, even at this time, reflection on the points that have been made, particularly in relation to the individual's own clinical setting, may help to make them more 'real'. Each one of us is in a position to challenge our own practice and ask questions about such things as the identification of standards within our area or the relationship of actions to tradition or knowledge. The questioning mind that is required of the skilled practitioner is sometimes hard to live with but, at the end of the day, seeing practice develop makes it all worth while.

3
Achieving Work

It has already been suggested that, in order to meet the changing demands of society, we must consider the way in which nursing work is managed. The shift in emphasis from a service centred on the cure or control of disease to a personalised service centred on people and their health has been discussed. However, it is also recognised that other factors are involved which have a significant role to play.

As far back as the 1960s, Menzies (1960) suggested that nurses used task-centred approaches to work intentionally as a mechanism for avoiding the anxiety created by involvement with patients. Davies' (1976) work, more than a decade later, suggested that there had been little change over that period. However, more recent work has suggested that denying people the opportunity to form close relationships with clients in fact denies them the support which can be gained in this way (Benner, 1984). Such comments must have implications for the way in which nursing work is managed.

The advent of a systematic approach to care, the so-called 'nursing process', has brought about some changes, but the emphasis in its introduction has been towards individualised care for patients with little attention paid to the management of nursing work as a whole in order to facilitate the change. A notable exception has been the work of Pembrey (1980), the central issue in her study being the relationship between management of work and individualised care. Pembrey argues that before considering how nursing can best be managed it is necessary to 'explore the nature of work in organisations'. She has used the work of Brown and Jacques (1965) as a framework for describing how work is achieved and applied it within the nursing world.

DESCRIBING WORK

Many people confine their view of work to physical activity, the 'doing' component and, indeed, there is a strong ethos in nursing that if you are not 'doing' you are not working (Figure 3.1).

Fig 3.1   An outcome of physical work alone??!

However, work can be described more accurately as a process with various stages. It may be seen as a series of activities through which we progress in order to achieve a certain aim. Three distinct stages can be identified:

Mental effort ⟶ Action ⟶ Observable outcomes

The 'mental effort' stage of work is the decision-making stage where all the factors which are relevant are taken into account. Brown and Jacques (1965) call this part of the process the 'exercise of discretion'. It is concerned with making choices about how the activity will be performed. In order to be able to exercise discretion effectively, people must be able to use their own judgment and have a known degree of freedom in which tc do so. However, this freedom can in itself place some strain on the individual concerned, the amount of strain being related to:

- *The authority a person has to work*   For example, in order to be able to exercise discretion about when to share information with a patient, the nurse must know whether he or she has authority over this aspect of work.
- *The number of choices or options available*   For instance, taking the same example further, the nurse may have to decide whether the relatives should be present during the discussion, how much the patient wants to know, what 'language' he will understand best, and so forth.

- *The degree of certainty about the outcome*   In this instance, the nurse may be unsure about how the patient will respond to the discussion.

In some circumstances, the amount of strain involved in the 'mental effort' component of work may be very small. Giving someone the apparently simple task of taking a temperature may seem straightforward. However, even in these circumstances difficulties can arise. First of all, if the individual does not have the correct knowledge, problems can occur either because there is no awareness of the factors which could influence the procedure, in this case such things as recent exercise, a hot bath or a cold drink, or because there is no understanding of the outcome. Thus, he or she will not be in a position to interpret the results, and anxiety can be created by not knowing if the resultant reading is within acceptable limits. The importance of these points lies in deciding who should be responsible for different aspects of work and then of making clear to that person the boundaries within which the outcomes are acceptable or when change should be reported.

The 'doing' stage of work is the action which is undertaken once the mental effort stage is completed. In relation to taking temperatures, it occurs once the decision has been made on which site to use, when to take the recording, how long to leave the thermometer in position, and so forth; it is the visible action phase. Some nurses are critical, particularly of their colleagues in management positions, of the delay in taking action. In some cases such criticism may be justified yet, from the example given, it can be seen that ignoring or paying insufficient attention to the mental effort stage of work can have serious consequences.

The 'observable outcome' stage of work is the end-product. In the temperature-taking example, it would be new knowledge about a named patient's temperature at a given time. The observable outcome is clear and easily identified. In other circumstances it is less clear and can cause anxiety, and thus an extra strain of work. For example, asking someone who is unsure of her ability to perform a task to continue with it will create great anxiety for that person. However, not allowing people room to exercise discretion within their personal abilities can be equally inappropriate as they will rapidly become frustrated and bored.

CAPACITY FOR WORK

'Capacity' is the word which has been used to describe people's ability to carry out work. It is concerned not only with the knowledge and skills required to perform the work, but also with the 'ability to use them effectively which is demonstrated in work performance' (Pembrey, 1980). Thus, an individual's capacity for work can be judged both by the ability to undertake a task in a protected environment or to demonstrate the knowledge, and by the ability to carry out that task in a work environment where the strain caused by the need to exercise discretion is also present (Figure 3.2).

It is important that there is a match between an individual's capacity for work and the work she or he is actually asked to perform; however, in reality, this is not always the case. For example, if students are asked to perform tasks for which they have not yet acquired the necessary knowledge, the anxiety created in an attempt to exercise discretion can be considerable. Similarly, if they do not know what the outcome of the work will be, they cannot judge whether their efforts have been appropriate, and considerable energy can be wasted in worrying about whether the work was satisfactory.

Alternatively, there are some people whose capacity for work is considerably bigger than their work role. We have all experienced the frustration of being able to see an appropriate course of action but not having the authority to act without first seeking permission. This is a fairly typical characteristic of a bureaucracy, where very rigid rules are laid down about the way in which a job can be performed with little room for an individual to exercise discretion. The result is often the set routines we see so frequently in a clinical environment, such as the timing of baths, to be completed before ten in the morning, or that all patients will wear nightclothes in hospital when this is not really necessary. Similarly, nurses' uncertainty about the degree of authority they have to impart information to patients may be a contributory factor in the

Fig 3.2 A thinker and a doer

avoidance of effective communication so widely reported (e.g. Faulkner, 1980). In order to overcome this sort of difficulty it is essential to make clear the boundaries of each person's work role and ensure that these match that person's capacity for work. Allowing people freedom to work independently once their capacity for work has been ensured has significant implications for the way in which managers work. The rigid hierarchical lines have to be loosened in order to allow room for the necessary freedom, and a shift towards a facilitative role rather than a directive one is required. This issue is discussed further in Part II (Chapter 13).

WORKING IN ORGANISATIONS

The purpose of an organisation is to bring together a group of people so that they can work together towards the achievement of mutual goals or aims. In order to achieve this, each person has a work role which contributes to the whole effort. In reality, this is not always the case and different members of an organisation may have sub-goals which are not mutually supportive and may even be antagonistic.

Part of the work of the leader of an organisation is to ensure that the resources, in terms of people, are used effectively in order to meet the organisational goals. Thus, the leader is concerned with differentiating between the content of different work roles, and then matching these with the people available, according to their capacity for work. In this way they can all pull together.

Following on from this description, either a ward, a health centre or a clinic can be taken as a complete organisation in its own right, even though it is part of a much larger organisational network. Within such a setting the leader must ensure that all the people:

- Aim towards the same goals
- Know what part they have to play
- Know the boundaries of their roles, which may be adjusted according to capacity
- Are given clear authority to act within those boundaries

One way of dealing with this situation is to clarify the 'norms' or expectations applied to each role, ensure that everyone knows those norms and then match people according to their individual capacities. Professional qualifications are obviously a good starting point in clarifying people's capacity. For example, the knowledge from which judgments are made about which action to take, and the ability to predict the outcomes of those actions, is initially gained through professional education. Using these criteria, it is obviously unjust to ask people with different backgrounds to make the same kind of judgments about how they should complete their work. Thus, it becomes unacceptable to ask the same things of a registered and an enrolled nurse, since their ability to exercise discretion, based on knowledge, is different. In the same way, newly-registered nurses will not have gained the same confidence in exercising their discretion as the experienced nurse, yet we often ask the same of them.

The other side of this coin is that it is equally important for people to be allowed freedom to exercise their discretion within the boundaries of their knowledge. If work is bound by rigid rules and procedures, the mental effort component will become lost. Not only is this frustrating for the incumbent of the role, but it is also ineffective since nothing gets done outside the predictable areas of work. While this may be satisfactory in a stable environment, such as a factory where the throughput of work is very controlled, its use is very questionable when the environment is often turbulent and variable, as is the case in a clinical setting. Moreover, if we profess to value personalised care, even though the desired outcomes may be predictable, the manner in which they are achieved must be flexible enough to match the individuality of the people concerned.

The use of performance review (Chapter 7) is another way of helping to identify people's capacity for work to the benefit of both themselves and those they work with. The use of a system of this type allows for individual development, taking advantage of people's strengths and supporting them in weak areas while safeguarding patients against the chance of the wrong person being asked to do the wrong job.

In order to achieve these ends, there are some basic principles which have to be clarified initially:

- The goals of the unit must be clear
- The boundaries of the role must be well defined
- People must be given authority to carry out their own work
- People must be given sufficient room to 'exercise discretion', provided that mutual goals are met

Thus, registered nurses may be given the authority to plan and implement all the care required by a named group of patients, including discharge planning and contact with other members of the care team and with the relatives, since their education has prepared them to do so. They will be allowed freedom to decide how this will be achieved provided it is within the overall framework of the unit.

In contrast, an unqualified or new member of the team may be asked to provide care for a patient but will be given precise instructions on how that care will be delivered and the parameters beyond which any changes should be reported. Obviously, the boundaries are much tighter.

This principle can also be applied to relatives who would like to become involved in helping with some aspects of care. They are often very unsure about what they are allowed to do, or indeed what is safe, and they do not always feel free to ask. However, it is quite possible for nurses to offer them the opportunity to clarify the 'boundaries', often with the result that they become very helpful members of the care team.

A word about goals, particularly as we are at the stage where there is so much change in nursing. It is essential that the overall goals of nursing within the unit are made clear to everyone since they will influence the way in which work is organised. If this is not done, great confusion can result. Consider one nurse who may believe that 'all the work should be completed by 10 o'clock, in case there is an emergency', while another may believe that personalised care means that there should be more flexibility in the timing; such a situation will almost inevitably lead to conflict (Figure 3.3).

Similarly, one nurse may see the purpose of her work as doing things FOR patients whilst another may see patient involvement

Fig 3.3 To do or not to do . . .

as being essential; again, there is potential for conflict. Such situations can be avoided by ensuring that all the people in the unit are clear about the overall beliefs and goals identified within the conceptual framework (Figure 3.4).

Fig 3.4   A shared goal

MANAGING

So what are the implications for those who are responsible for managing nursing work? Management can be described as the 'art of getting work done through people'. Management, like work or many other things, can also be considered as a process with a series of steps which, although interrelated, can be described separately. Four are usually described, those of planning, organising, leading and controlling.

Planning

The first task of any manager is to define the goals or objectives which are being sought by the organisation. If, as would be the case of someone managing a clinical unit, that person is responsible for a sub-unit within a larger organisation, the local goals must be compatible with the goals of the whole organisation. In other words, the manager of a clinical nursing unit should not identify goals which are at variance with health authority policy. They must be realistic and planned within the resources available. It would be unrealistic to say that every patient would have the sole attention of a nurse at all times, nor would it be necessary. However, at a clinical level, it may be agreed that the broad goal is to ensure that the highest quality nursing service possible will be provided for patients within the resources available. (This does not mean to say that more resources cannot be asked for, provided that the request can be justified.) But since different people will interpret such a statement in different ways it is necessary to be much more specific. For instance, it could be suggested that the goal of the unit is to help patients to achieve the maximum level of independence in the shortest possible time. This would obviously not be compatible with the views of those nurses who believe that, as described earlier, their job is to do everything for patients.

The need to share a conceptual image of nursing becomes even more apparent when such practice issues are recognised. The ability to conceptualise was raised in chapter 2. Further help can be gained in this area by studying the literature related to nursing models, where views of the broad goals of nursing are explored.

Forecasting

In order to be able to plan, an effective manager must have sufficient information to be able to *forecast*. This is important in terms both of the amount and the type of work to be undertaken, and of the resources which will be available. Resource information may include the number and grade of staff, their holiday allowances, predictable shortfalls, patterns of patient throughput, average bed occupancy or case-load, and the type of patient problems with which the nursing staff will be involved. With this information at hand, plans can be made for future action which take maximum advantage of the opportunities available while minimising the risks. For example, by forecasting the number of weeks of annual leave which will be taken by all the staff of the unit, a steady flow of leave can be arranged rather than a sudden rush at peak holiday times or at the end of the financial year.

Organising Work

This stage of management is concerned with developing a structure which allows the plans to be implemented. In the past the most common style of organisation to be found in nursing was one based on the principles of 'scientific management' which can be attributed to Taylor (1947). This style is typified by a bureaucratic structure. To most people, bureaucracy is synonymous with 'red tape' and difficulty in getting things done. In fact, it is a very rigid, well-ordered form of organisation which, in some circumstances, can achieve the organisational objectives very effectively. The characteristics of a bureaucracy can be summarised as:

- A pyramidal shape with increasing authority and responsibility towards the top
- Rigid rules and regulations in order to control work
- Fixed and limited official duties
- Methodical division of labour and specialisation
- Impersonality of managers
- Promotion by merit of seniority and the ability to fulfil the current job
- Piecework and bonus schemes
- The major aim of meeting the organisational goals regardless of any human factors

This type of structure is still seen in many big organisations and certainly within the health service. Nursing has traditionally been structured in this way and most people will recognise elements of the approach in current practice. Although it can be argued that bureaucracies are efficient, they bring with them very specific difficulties: because the human element is ignored there tends to be a rapid turnover of staff as well as a high sickness rate; motivation to work is low and there is an inclination to stop when 'the boss' is absent.

It can be argued that a belief in the usefulness of bureaucratic structures is largely based on assumptions about what makes people work well. McGregor (1960) has described alternative theories of human nature, known as Theory X and Theory Y, which relate to this topic. The basic premises of Theory X are that most workers:

- Naturally dislike work and are lazy
- Therefore seek to avoid work
- Must be coerced, threatened or bribed in order to work
- Dislike, and will therefore seek to avoid, responsibility
- Lack initiative
- Prefer to be directed

If this description of people is felt to be true, the advantages of a bureaucratic organisation can clearly be seen. However, if on the one hand we say that care must be personalised to suit individual people and on the other suggest that nurses must work within a rigid set of rules with little opportunity to 'exercise individual discretion', we would be defeating our own ends.

McGregor's Theory Y offers an alternative view of people. It suggests that:

- Physical and mental effort in work is as natural as in play
- External control and threat of punishment are not the only means of bringing about effort. If committed, people will exercise self-direction and self-control in working towards objectives
- Commitment to objectives is related to the rewards associated with their fulfilment
- The average person learns, under proper conditions, not only to accept, but to seek, responsibility
- The capacity to exercise a relatively high degree of imagination, ingenuity and creativity in solving problems is widely not narrowly distributed in the population
- The intellectual potential of most human beings is only partly used

If these views are accepted, the rigidity of a bureaucratic style of work organisation is then no longer acceptable and the school of thought known as the *human relations approach* can be brought into play. This approach recognises that social and psychological factors can have a stronger influence on commitment to work than does economic reward alone. It lays emphasis on the importance of human interactions as a means of increasing morale.

The work of Herzberg (1959) can be useful in making decisions about how to manage work. He identified two separate but important areas which have to be taken into account as factors which influence people's potential to work effectively. They are known as the *hygiene* and the *motivator* factors.

Hygiene factors are concerned with such issues as salary, personal relationships with colleagues, status, work conditions, job security, quality of supervision and company policies and practice. If there are difficulties in any of these areas, Herzberg suggests that there can be a negative effect on an individual's work performance. However, satisfaction in all these areas does not necessarily mean that people will be fulfilled and, therefore, committed to their work. It is the so-called 'motivator' factors which can lead to this end. Motivator factors include:

- Achievement – the opportunity to complete work satisfactorily
- Recognition of work
- The content of the work

- Responsibility for one's own work
- Opportunity for advancement

So, how can these ideas influence the way in which work is organised? Several general principles can be elicited.

1. People need to know what the goals of work are in order that they know what they are working towards. Thus, each clinical unit needs to make a clear and public statement about what it is trying to achieve.

2. The roles of each team member, or the expectations of each person, must be clarified according to his individual capacity to work. Thus, people should not be asked to undertake work which is beyond their capacity through either lack of knowledge or of the ability to use that knowledge.

3. Boundaries should be made explicit in order that people know when they have the authority to act independently and when they need to refer back to others.

4. There should be an opportunity to see the whole cycle of work through, including the outcome of practice. If a sense of achievement is to be gained, nurses need to see the same patients throughout their whole need for nursing rather than changing patient groups every day.

5. Once work has been allocated, people need to be allowed freedom to fulfil that work independently and according to their own judgment. They need to be allowed to 'get on with the job in hand' rather than be watched continuously with interference from the supervisor.

6. People need the opportunity for regular feedback in order both to learn and to gain recognition for their work.

While it is important that the so called hygiene factors, such as salary, conditions of service and so forth, are satisfactory, they are not sufficient to ensure that people will be committed to their work. Ignoring the motivator factors can lead to an unhappy and frustrated workforce who, in consequence, do not give of their best.

Leadership

Leadership has been described as 'the wise use of power' (Claus and Bailey, 1977): it is the ability to influence others effectively in order to accomplish a goal. Much work has been undertaken over the years to try to identify what makes an effective leader, yet it is an elusive thing to define. It used to be suggested that leaders were 'born' rather than 'made' and possessed specific personality traits, yet no firm conclusions could be reached since the characteristics were so varied.

An alternative approach was that anyone can become a leader in a given set of circumstances if he or she possesses the greatest knowledge of the situation but, again, this idea was found to be unsatisfactory since not everyone can rise to the occasion.

The *transactional approach* to leadership proposed by Fielder (1967) attempts to marry previous ideas, the suggestion being that leadership is, in fact, a reciprocal approach of social influence in which leaders both influence followers and are influenced by them.

Leadership Styles

There are three basic kinds of leadership style which have commonly been described: the autocrat or authoritarian, the democrat and the permissive or 'laissez faire' leader.

Autocratic Leadership   The autocratic leader is essentially exploitive and, in extreme forms, will use the efforts of the workers to the best possible advantage of the employer with no regard what so ever for their well-being. Such a style is commonly seen in a rigid organisation where work is allocated in part-task form and the structure is bureaucratic in nature. If McGregor's Theory X (see above) is accepted, this would then be an appropriate style of leadership. However, it has been suggested that McGregor's picture of autocratic leadership is too harsh and workers *are* considered, but they *need* structure and discipline. Thus, the *benevolent autocrat* emerges, one who is paternalistic and caring but allows no freedom (Figure 3.5).

Permissive Leadership   Some people will argue that this is no style of leadership since it is totally permissive, giving no direction to the workers. Power is relinquished to the followers, who are given total freedom.

Such a style can be recognised in some clinical areas where there is no leadership or direction. Everyone 'gets on with the job together'. No boundaries are set and it is unclear who is responsible for which aspects of work. While there are a few areas where such a style may be appropriate, such as amongst a group of research scientists, it is potentially disastrous in an organisation such as a

Fig 3.5 The benevolent autocrat

hospital or health centre. Since no common goals are set and no-one is sure what is expected of him, there is every chance that some areas of work will be omitted while others will be done twice. On the whole, it is not an appropriate style to consider in a clinical unit.

Democratic Leadership   The essential characteristic of democratic leadership is that it is 'people-orientated' and encourages a participative approach. Communication is open and trusting in both directions. Goals are jointly identified for the good of all. This may mean that they do not suit each person all the time but it is recognised by all that there is a common cause.

An example of differing leadership styles may be seen in nursing by the way the off-duty rota is prepared. The autocratic leader will stipulate exactly when each individual will work, with no concern for personal needs, whilst the 'laissez faire' leader will grant all requests regardless of ward cover with a nonchalant 'We'll manage somehow'! The democratic leader will look at the needs of the individual, and of the unit and try to match the two. This may mean that each person's 'ideal' duty rota cannot always be met but at least others will not be left in impossible situations because the unit is inadequately covered.

Some of the basic theories which can be helpful in planning ward work have been introduced in this chapter but these give only a taste of some of the ideas that can be drawn on. Recommendations for further reading will be found at the end of Part I (after Chapter 4) and it is strongly recommended that these be followed up.

4
Job Analysis and the Organisation of Care

Before a decision can be made about which is the best way of getting a job done, the overall aims of both nursing and the whole health-care team must be considered. The manner in which the work is undertaken must reflect health promotion, consideration of the individuality of people, the environment in which they live and work and the use of a systematic approach.

In the light of these aims there are two major issues to be considered in relation to the management and organisation of work: first, job analysis and, second, working relationships. Each will be considered separately although they are closely related.

JOB ANALYSIS

Job analysis requires the collection of data which will reveal the nature and characteristics of the work being undertaken in an identified situation (Figure 4.1). In relationship to nursing work, information needs to be collected in the following areas:

- The personal characteristics, health status and environment of the client or client group being served
- The method of work being used
- The aims of the total health service
- The aims of nursing and the standards expected
- Nursing staff, both those available and those required to do the job
- Time
- Available budget
- Organisational constraints
- Legislation, local policy and procedures
- The work of other disciplines
- The volume of work generated by and for the organisation

Some of the areas identified as being relevant to job analysis are expanded briefly here and some are discussed more fully in Part II of the book.

Fig 4.1 What's in a job?

Personal Characteristics, Health Status and Environment

Data may be collected about the physical and psychosocial characteristics of the client groups served, their health status and the environment both in which they live and where they receive nursing. From this data, it may be possible to identify trends or characteristics which would be useful in forward planning. For example, if a large proportion of the client group served is elderly, even though the unit is not designated especially for this purpose, it may be worth thinking of including in the team a nurse who has gained specialist skills in this area who could act as a consultant to the other team members.

Similarly, if a large proportion of the patients comes from less affluent areas, it could be worth while keeping information about access to assistance, with the relevant telephone numbers to hand.

Much of this information is already available but rarely used at clinical level. For example, a ward admissions book coupled with information from district statistics can reveal such things as the age range of clients, the commonest age group receiving care, the range of areas in which they live, the types of occupation they undertake, the average length of stay in hospital and the clinical diagnoses. It could include information about the reasons for needing care, which may be for nursing, social or medical needs. All this information can be used in helping to identify the knowledge and skills required both by someone working with clients and for future planning.

The type of information sought and the way in which it is analysed are determined by the conceptual framework of the unit, in particular the 'ingredients' of nursing discussed in Chapter 2. The framework clarifies those things which are important to nursing and upon which nursing decisions are made.

Work Method

The method of work relates to the final concept central to nursing discussed in Chapter 2, the recommended method being that of a systematic approach based on the action research model, which will help to answer nursing questions or identify solutions for nursing problems. Seven basic components were considered. From an analysis of each activity there are indications as to who can reasonably be held accountable for each one. Each activity inherently requires a certain degree of knowledge, skill and attitudes for its fulfilment. For example, in the first activity, data relating to the nursing situation is collected and analysed, which obviously requires the ability to perceive what information is required, the discrimination to judge when to collect the information and the skill to elicit that information.

In order to ensure that this activity is undertaken successfully the following questions must be asked and answered:

- Who should be accountable for the decision on what data it is appropriate to collect?
- Who is the fit and proper person with the necessary knowledge, skills and attitudes to collect that data?
- Who can, and should, make sense of the data?

Asking someone who does not have the necessary ability to 'exercise discretion' in this situation is unfair and unethical to both the nurse and the client. The identified work method chosen has far-reaching implications for deciding the background of the nurse needed to do the job.

Aims of the Total Health Service

In recent times the move has been towards a more personalised service or, as it is often referred to, individualised care. Over the last few years, the actual meaning of these words seems to have been lost in the turmoil and confusion of change. This may be an appropriate time to review and re-establish what we actually mean by such a statement. Many nurses have confused the notion of a personalised or individual service with the use of the nursing process. The nursing process is a method of work which, at best, will only facilitate the establishment of a personalised service. It says nothing of the 'ingredients' of nursing, but is merely a work method.

So what is a personalised service? The following might be considered indicators of such a service:

- The separate and unique identity of each person is maintained
- It is people who are important and of consequence and their individuality is not superseded by the disease which may have altered their health status
- Licence to express individuality or personality through dress, acquisition of personal belongings and habits of daily living is given
- There is the opportunity for clients to contribute to the plans for their own care
- Clients are in receipt of information which allows them to make informed decisions about their own care

There are many overt ways in which some of these indicators may be seen at a clinical level. For example, in many units all the clients are expected to wear their nightclothes throughout their stay whereas they may well be more comfortable in day wear. Examination of the information collected during assessment may give a clue to the balance between disease-related data and information which will help to personalise care. The number of people to whom each patient has to relate during his stay may indicate the degree of opportunity he has to contribute to planning. The examples could be endless but these are just a few specific indicators which may be helpful.

The implications of providing a personalised service are far-reaching and may influence the following factors:

- The method of work chosen
- The nurse–patient relationship
- The organisational structure
- Distribution of power
- Distribution of resources
- Education
- Professional ideologies
- Organisational procedures and policy-making

The Aims of Nursing and Nursing Standards

The aims of nursing must obviously coincide with the overall aims of the service. Review of the conceptual framework which has been selected will assist in the clarification of a personalised service, since the overall aim should be made clear within it. It will also help to identify certain standards related to the values to be upheld and the rights to be acknowledged. These standards can be facilitated through the method of work used, the nurse–client relationship and the implementation of therapeutic nursing.

Both the identification and the upholding of nursing standards are the responsibility of all nurses, ranging from the statutory body to each individual who has the right to be called a nurse. The standards identified cannot be influenced or altered on a day-to-day basis by organisational constraints such as the availability of staff and other resources, although such issues may make it more difficult to achieve them at some times than at others. Standards, however, must be open to modification or change in the light of professional developments and social change.

Available and Required Staff

By the overall consideration of a given situation it is possible to gain a clear picture of individual work roles, thus facilitating the identification of the types of people who can fill the roles most appropriately. For example, if a need to make discriminative decisions about nursing actions is identified, it is obviously inappropriate to place an unqualified person in that particular position. However, it should also be borne in mind that the constraints of such things as budget size and organisational policies must always be taken into account.

The number and quality of staff required to do the job must be ascertained within realistic terms. Methods of measuring nursing work in terms of the number of nurses required to do the job have been described in several studies (DHSS, 1984, Figure 4.2). These are commonly referred to as 'dependency studies'. Many of these methods are elaborate, time-consuming and procedure-centred, although more recent ones have attempted to move towards a more person-centred approach (e.g. Telford, 1979). However, care must still be taken when applying the techniques, which are essentially quantitative in nature, to a person-centred service which has a large qualitative component. The choice of dependency tool should always be influenced by such consider-ations, bearing in mind the balance between the organisation's need for efficiency and the professional ideology.

Hitherto, great emphasis has been placed on numbers, with almost total disregard for the mix or qualities of the staff required. There is little evidence available to give formal guidance when

Fig 4.2 Measuring nursing work

planning the appropriate 'staff mix' for a unit. However, once an analysis of the work has been undertaken it becomes easier to match that work with the capacity that people have to undertake it, by virtue of their qualifications and experience.

Time

Time, or the lack of it, is much maligned as being the cause of poor work. Time is a fixed commodity, a minute is a minute, an hour is an hour, and cannot be shortened or lengthened. However, if we complain about the lack of time we must be absolutely sure that we are making the best possible use of the time which is available and not spending it in the performance of work which is either inappropriate to nursing or routinised and habitual rather than planned. So what is the actual problem? One solution may be to look at the actual work practices themselves which may make poor use of time. Some work practices which may influence the efficient use of time include:

- Methods of nursing
- Assignment of staff
- Duty rotas
- Methods of communication

Methods of Nursing

It is argued by some that a systematic approach to nursing is too time-consuming; for example, the value of making an appropriate assessment of a situation does not warrant the time taken. However, it can also be argued that, by making such an assessment, only the work which needs to be done is undertaken, thereby saving time in the long run. It is also a factor which contributes to the overall quality of the service by identifying what the client wants and needs. Furthermore, thorough assessment can in many instances highlight potential problems which, if not avoided before they become actual problems, can lead to the need for further time-consuming activities at a later date.

A 'routine and custom' approach to care, in contrast, assures instant activity on the part of the workers, since learned routines can be put into practice immediately on presentation of an appropriate situation. However, such routines are frequently only related to the medical diagnosis, the prescribed medical treatment, or simply the entry into or exit from the care system. As these points do not relate personally to the individual client, it is highly likely that some of the work done may be irrelevant or inappropriate for a particular person.

Assignment of Staff

The need to match people's work to their actual ability has already been discussed in Chapter 3. If work is allocated inappropriately, there can be two serious outcomes: first, the senior nurse may be interrupted by a less experienced colleague who is overanxious because she or he does not have the 'capacity' to undertake the work assigned; and, second, an inexperienced person may have insufficient knowledge to be able to recognise changes in circumstances, responses to care or choices of action.

Duty Rotas

Hours to be worked are negotiated at a national level. However, how these hours are worked is a local matter, local being taken to mean at team or individual practitioner level, and they must reflect the demand and the need. Often there is a policy within a hospital about shift times and duty rotas, yet what is appropriate for one ward may be quite inappropriate for another.

If nurses are to deliver a personalised service, a much more flexible approach to working hours is needed. By using a systematic approach it is possible to predict peaks and troughs in the demand for nursing within individual units and to plan the duty rotas accordingly (see Chapter 11).

This flexibility of working hours does not fit into the bureaucratic style of organisation seen so frequently in the health-care system. Opposition has been and will be met when proposing such changes to work practices; indeed, many nurses are themselves resistant to changes in the shift patterns with which they are familiar. However, flexibility can be beneficial to both staff and clients and, in this day of economic constraint, it is something which must be considered.

Methods of Communication

Traditionally, the main means of communication among nurses about clients has been verbal. Written communication has tended to be incomplete, inaccurate, held in low esteem by nurses and considered to be a waste of time. How often have colleagues been heard to complain about all the time wasted with 'unnecessary writing' when they could be with patients? Arguments about the documentation of nursing remain heated. To help to resolve the debate it is helpful to explore:

- What is to be communicated
- Why it must be communicated
- The methods that are available and their strengths and weaknesses
- Technological aids available

The human memory is not infallible: things are forgotten and information is lost, misinterpreted or misheard. Yet we are all aware of the potential inaccuracies which can occur when we rely on verbal communication alone. With these points in mind it should be possible to select the most appropriate method for each situation, taking advantage of both the modern technology available, such as computer print-outs of admissions and discharges, and of an understanding of the effectiveness of different methods of sharing information. These issues are discussed more fully in a later chapter but it is worth noting here that increased efficiency can be achieved through the use of new technological developments both in the area of therapeutic nursing and in communication.

ORGANISATION OF CARE

It is necessary to make a clear distinction between the structure, or organisation, of nursing work and the methods or activities used to deliver nursing. A structure itself is not a method of nursing – it is simply a means of organising staff to use a method.

There are two main structures currently recognised and practised in nursing, namely *primary nursing* and *team nursing*. Primary nursing is a total system in its own right and stands alone. Team nursing can be associated with two alternative sub-systems, namely task allocation and patient/client allocation. In some units, primary nurses each have a specific group of nurses or care-givers working with them who together form a team, but it is important to differentiate this from the concept of 'team' nursing described below. Another term which is widely used is that of 'total patient care'. This expression can be subsumed into the terms 'patient allocation' or 'primary nursing' as it is inherent in both these systems.

The choice of a system, and appropriate sub-systems, will depend largely on the outcome of the job analysis which, in itself, relates to the identification of a conceptual framework. Different combinations of the main system with sub-systems will, however, facilitate different degrees of personalisation of the service, as shown in Figure 4.3.

The key to a personalised service is continuity, for continuity of relationships facilitates the way in which the people concerned get to know each other, the establishment of trust and confidence, accountability of the nurse to the client and effective communication. Continuity must, however, be considered in terms of both the nurse–nurse working relationship and the nurse–client relationship.

Primary Nursing

This is a system which is best described in relation to the role of the primary nurse. In this approach to the organisation of nursing, clients are allocated to a primary nurse when they first enter the care system. The primary nurse then holds sole responsibility for their nursing as long as the need continues, on a 24-hours-a-day, seven-days-a-week basis.

Since the primary nurse is seen as a professional practitioner who is both responsible and accountable for the nursing a client receives, it is totally unacceptable that anyone without qualification as a registered nurse should undertake the role. Indeed, the

Level of personalisation	System combination			
I N C R E A S I N G P E R S O N A L I S A T I O N	Task allocation	to task teams	Task allocation to team members for whole patient group	
	Patient allocation	to patient teams	Task allocation to team members for team-patient group only	
	Patient allocation	to patient teams	Patient allocation to individual team members	Total patient care while on duty
	Patient allocation	to primary nurse	Total patient care for entire need for nursing	

Fig 4.3 The degree of personalised service

incumbent should ideally be a nurse who has had considerable experience. The role makes heavy demands on the individual concerned and also provides the opportunity for a great deal of job satisfaction. At present in many hospitals, the availability of suitably prepared nurses is limited and this is one of the factors which prevents the system from being adopted more widely. However, some units are moving steadily towards this approach.

In the community setting the situation is quite different. The majority of community nursing staff have attained a second qualification prior to working outside the safe confines of the hospital. In some instances this is a statutory requirement, and by means of this regulation more suitably qualified staff are available. The current system of organising care in the community is the one which most closely resembles primary nursing and is not too far removed from the nurse practitioner role envisaged in the Cumberlege Report (DHSS, 1986).

When a primary nurse is off duty, the nursing she has prescribed is given by another nurse, known as an 'associate' (Elhart et al, 1978). The associate nurse may be another primary nurse, with her own clients, who provides cover during a colleague's absence. Alternatively, the associate nurse may be another nurse who is assigned to the primary nurse to work alongside her as a member of a team (Figure 4.4).

This latter method is an ideal way of incorporating enrolled nurses into the primary nursing system. It is also a very appropriate role for a newly-registered nurse who has not yet had the experience to take on the full responsibilities of a primary nurse. Similarly, those nurses who only work part-time, and are therefore not available for a sufficient length of time to gain the continuity needed in order to be a primary nurse, can act as associates.

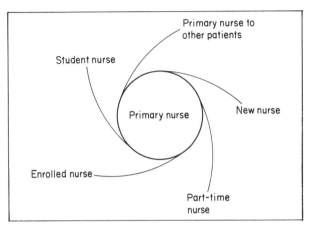

Fig 4.4   Primary and associate nurses

It is recognised that, at certain times, it may be necessary to make alterations in the primary nurse's plan for the well-being of the client. It is perfectly acceptable for the associate to make changes in such circumstances although obviously she would later have to justify the need for alterations to the primary nurse. In reality, most situations can be predicted and therefore contingency plans to meet them can be made by the primary nurse. On rare occasions, the primary nurse may ask to be contacted if a particular situation arises when she is not on duty; however, from the experience of those who practise this approach, this is a rare occurrence and can usually be anticipated.

If a nurse thinks that primary nursing might be a suitable structure for organising nursing in her unit, a number of factors need to be thought about before a move is made in this direction. Consideration has to be given to:

1. *The number of primary nurses required*   This is dependent on the number of clients each one can accept responsibility for. The number is influenced by the degree of dependency of the clients, but as a general guide is thought to be about six (Manthey, 1978). Obviously, if the need for nursing is not very high, the number may be greater; in the same way, in high-dependency situations it may be lower.

2. *The qualities required of the primary nurse*   Ideally, this is not seen as a suitable role for a newly-registered nurse but for an 'expert' in the particular field of nursing, preferably with some postbasic qualification or, at the very least, experience beyond initial qualification.

3. *The relationship of the associate to the primary nurse*   This may be according to the availability of other staff or there may be a team of nurses specifically designated to work with one particular primary nurse.

4. *The qualities of the associate nurse*   This will depend on the nursing needs of the particular client group concerned, but may include a variety of people with different backgrounds and experience.

Should primary nursing be selected as the appropriate system of organising care, the method of work employed also has to be agreed and, as will doubtless have been realised, the one which we would recommend is a systematic approach, that is, the nursing process. It also follows that the primary nurse is responsible, and hence accountable, for all activities of nursing. However, the associate, in accepting responsibility for the delivery of nursing in the absence of the primary nurse is obviously accountable for his or her own actions.

Team Nursing

Team nursing can be described as a system where a group of people work together to complete nursing work by the organised division of labour. Those in the team co-operate and pull together to meet the identified aims and objectives. In the same way as with primary nursing, when choosing a team nursing structure it is necessary to consider:

- The number of teams required
- The number and qualities of team members
- The continuity of the team structure
- The leadership of the team
- The dynamics and philosophy of the team

The decision reached as to how teams should be formed can be based on the individual job analyses of the unit, a knowledge of the dynamics of relationships and the need for continuity in these relationships. Teams will obviously vary from one clinical situation to another. There is no hard and fast rule regarding their structure as it is based on the unique nature of the presenting situation. However, one should always be aware of the way in which the structuring of the team affects the personalisation of the service to clients, since some approaches are more efficient than others in this respect.

It must also be borne in mind that structures are constrained by finance and the most desirable approach, from a professional point of view, may not initially appear to be the one which is most economical or acceptable to the organisation. It is, therefore, necessary to be able to explain the reasoning behind a desired team structure in economic as well as professional terms. For example, it may be necessary to debate the issue of the quality of staff versus the quantity within the same budget. The initial work undertaken in the job analysis should be helpful in such a debate.

Ideally, each team should function as a discrete unit. However, during the current period of change within the health service where resources are low, it is necessary to show adaptability and flexibility in work practices. Teams may have to co-operate with each other, particularly in the implementation of nursing. For example, if a patient allocated to a team requires the assistance of two people to move him, and only one member of the team is available, obviously help would then be given from another team.

Individual members of a team may possess different qualities and capabilities in terms of statutory qualifications, further education, personality and life experience. It can be argued that there is a disproportionate mix of statutory qualifications and backgrounds in many nursing teams at the moment so that people of different abilities are expected to undertake the same work. Disproportion can occur either because of the number of members of a team who have no statutory qualification or because of the mix between registered and enrolled nurses. In many units the whole workforce acts as one big team with the sister or charge nurse acting as team leader. However, this gives little opportunity for other qualified members of the staff to 'exercise discretion' and gain both experience and job satisfaction. Furthermore, it is difficult for one person to have sufficient in-depth information about all the clients to be able to plan their care efficiently.

In other areas, the ward staff may be sub-divided into smaller teams with a designated leader other than the ward sister, and a named client group either allocated because of their position in the ward or, preferably, by matching the clients' needs with the skill of the team members. In the same way as with primary nursing, the team leader should always be a registered nurse since she is the one responsible for the nursing which is given.

The people working together in a team may stay together for fairly long periods of time; this is obviously the case when all the ward staff work together as one big team. Alternatively, the structure of the team may be altered on a regular basis, and in some units it is changed with each shift. This obviously creates some difficulties in both continuity of relationships with clients and in the leadership of the team. It can be very frustrating for staff since they are always having to learn to work with new people and are often put in the position of not seeing patients with whom they worked on a previous shift and, therefore, being unable to watch their progress. Similarly, it can be frustrating for patients since they can never get to know the nurses who are caring for them, often having to explain the same information over and over again.

There is still great confusion about who can fulfil the leadership role of a clinical nursing team. Again, job analysis will help to clarify the issue, since it will identify the appropriate knowledge, skills, attitudes and personality traits required of the leader. Much of the confusion arises from the current two-tier system which exists in British nursing, the use of people with different qualifications interchangeably and, to some extent, the unavailability of appropriately qualified personnel. There is also some conflict of interest between the organisation and the professional ideals, with a higher priority being given to quantity than to quality. However, when it is recognised that a team leader is responsible for the quality of nursing which a group of clients receives, and that nursing must be planned on a sound knowledge base, it becomes evident that only those who, at a minimum, are registered nurses should rightly be designated team leaders.

In the absence of the team leader, another member of the team may be designated to act on his or her behalf; alternatively, a team leader from another team may give cover for a short period of time. If the teams are reconstructed on a day-to-day basis, this problem does not arise, but neither does the team leader get the satisfaction of being really responsible for the continuing care of the clients or the relationship with colleagues.

Central to the team approach to care is the participation of all team members in all aspects of care, although the specific responsibility for some aspects may be vested in a particular team member. This is the essential difference between team nursing and primary nursing. If a team is attached to work alongside a primary nurse, all team members will be able to contribute but the responsibility for decision-making lies with the primary nurse alone.

There are, however, other ways by which teams may choose to organise their work – the sub-systems identified earlier. Each one is discussed below with both the advantages and disadvantages highlighted.

Sub-System A: Task Allocation

Task allocation is a well-known system of organising nursing work. It implies that a series of tasks is allocated to each nurse, such as taking temperatures or doing dressings and, in this way, each nurse knows exactly what he or she is responsible for. Similarly, the person in charge of the ward knows exactly who is responsible for the completion of the named tasks. However, there are several problems with this method of organising work. First, any tasks which have not been allocated do not get done, since it is the responsibility of no-one in particular to look for them and, more importantly, take on the responsibility for doing them. Consequently, changes in circumstances can often go unnoticed, especially if these are unexpected. Second, any tasks which have not been identified by the person in charge are not noticed or, if they are noticed, may not be responded to by other team members.

Third, clients may find that they are disturbed frequently by different nurses, each of whom has one aspect of their care to see to. Not only is this very disruptive but it can also be very confusing, for patients can be unsure whom they should give information to or ask for help. As a consequence, they either ask no-one or try to catch the attention of every nurse who goes by in order to ensure that attention is given to their difficulties.

Within team nursing, it is quite feasible to use a system of task allocation. Indeed, it is not uncommon for people to suggest that they are carrying out individualised care when in fact what they are doing is continuing to work to tasks, but for a smaller group of patients; thus, if there is more than one member of a team on duty, they divide the work between them by task rather than by patient. Such an approach holds all the risks which have already been identified in relation to this system.

Having been so critical of task allocation in relationship to nursing work, it must be said that it is a very efficient way of organising work in some situations. For example, when there is an emergency and things need to be done very quickly, allocating tasks to the people who are available to help can be very efficacious.

In the same way, there are some areas of ward work, not directly related to giving patient care but nevertheless essential to the smooth running of the ward, which can be allocated to individual nurses within the team very effectively. For example, it is essential in any clinical environment that the equipment is well-maintained. The task of checking individual items of equipment can be allocated to different team members according to their knowledge and experience; in the same way, a check can be kept on the storage of drugs, the completion of the duty rota or numerous other essential tasks. Indeed, if no named person is responsible for the completion of such activities they are just the sort of thing which can be neglected. Thus, it can be seen that while task allocation is not a very desirable way of organising clinical nursing work it should not be totally ignored as there are other aspects of work to which it can be applied very effectively.

Sub-System B: Patient Allocation

In many units it is now common practice to allocate individual patients to individual nurses, a system which has become known as patient allocation. Yet there are huge variations in the way in which this system is used in practice. In some cases, the allocation takes place on a daily basis, the senior nurse on duty assigning patients to nurses at the beginning of each shift. This is one way of ensuring that there is always an assigned person responsible for each patient and that nurses know what their responsibilities are for the shift. Some people will also argue that it is a way of ensuring that nurses have a variety of experience in their work situation and the problem of 'overinvolvement' or personality clashes is overcome.

While the rationale for such arguments can be seen, they must be considered in the light of other issues. The importance of the nurse–patient relationship has been continuously highlighted and a change of allocation on a daily basis in no way facilitates the development of such a relationship, putting extra demands on both the patient and the nurse. While it is acknowledged that from time to time there will be a clash of personalities between the two people concerned, our experience suggests that this is a rare occurrence. The longer the relationship lasts, the greater is the understanding of the people involved and, hence, their ability to work together. However, it would be unrealistic to expect all people to be able to get on well together and any system should be flexible enough to allow for changes should such a situation arise.

There is a more important issue, however, namely the need for any worker to be able to see the outcome of his or her labours. If allocation of patients is changed on a day-to-day basis, there is no opportunity for the nurse to see the progress of a patient, nor does she have the chance to see whether the care which has been given is successful in helping the patient to move towards the identified goals. So, while patient allocation certainly has advantages over task allocation in relation to patient care, allocation on a day-to-day basis loses some of the benefits of this system. There is no doubt that within a clinical setting there are times when flexibility is needed and it may be necessary to alter allocations but, on the whole, the advantages of allocation over a number of shifts far outweigh the difficulties.

The major difference between patient allocation over several days on a team basis and primary nursing lies in accountability for the nursing. With patient allocation the accountability for the provision of care is passed to the next team member at the change of each shift. However, with primary nursing the accountability is retained by the primary nurse even in his or her absence, and changes in nursing prescription are only made in an emergency. We will leave it to the reader to consider which is a more fulfilling way of working from both the patients' and the nurses' perspective; however, we suspect that our preferences are apparent.

The Role of the Ward Sister or Charge Nurse

The traditional role of the ward sister or charge nurse was one where responsibilities included those of both clinical nurse and general manager of the ward. The operational structure was hierarchical in nature and the ward sister the pivot around which everything ran: she was the keeper of all information and the director of all activity. In either of the two systems described above, the situation is fundamentally different (unless there is only one team retained in one ward). The question must then be raised as to where the ward sister fits into such a structure.

It must be stressed that the role of the sister remains vital within either structure, although her function may well be different from the one which we have known traditionally. In order to save confusion it may, therefore, be helpful to consider another title such as 'clinical ward leader', or just 'senior nurse'. However, many people prefer to stay with the familiar title and there is no reason why this should not be the case, provided that the different functions are made clear.

So, if the responsibility for the planning and delivery of nursing is delegated to either the team leader or the primary nurse, what does the sister or charge nurse actually do? There are several areas of responsibility which have always been within his or her remit which have not in the past always been developed to the full. These include:

- Clarification of the conceptual framework from which the practice of the ward arises
- General management of the ward, including control of the ward budget. This is particularly important with the advent of the Griffiths structure (1984)
- Acting as clinical nursing consultant to other members of the nursing staff
- Developing expertise in a particular area of nursing in order to act as a specialist
- Responsibility for staff appraisal and development
- Research from a clinical base
- The educational experience of students

The list could be endless as there are so many areas which relate directly to practice but which so often are left undone, either because the time is not available or they are not given priority. Yet the omission of any of the areas mentioned above can have serious consequences for the smooth running of the ward. People work towards different goals, they do not know whether or not their work is satisfactory, staff development can be neglected or unco-ordinated so that some colleagues get out of date, and so forth. Just from these brief comments one can see the essential role that the ward sister/charge nurse has to play in either of these two systems.

In this chapter, different ways of organising nursing work have been introduced. There are advantages and disadvantages to any system but it is important to weigh one against another before deciding which is most appropriate in any one place. Sometimes it can take many months, or even years, to move from one way of working to another, and people should not be disheartened if progress seems slow. It is often better to move a little way well than to try to change the world in a day. Nevertheless, careful consideration of the sort of system which may be thought to facilitate the best service for patients and a slow, well-planned movement towards that system are worth working for.

Suggested Further Reading for Part I

Benner P (1984) *From Novice to Expert: Excellence and Power in Clinical Nursing.* Reading MA: Addison-Wesley.

Bond J and Bond S (1986) *Sociology and Health Care. An Introduction for Nurses and other Health Care Professionals.* Edinburgh: Churchill Livingstone.

Bowman M (1986) *Nursing Management and Education: A Conceptual Approach to Change.* London: Croom Helm.

Calnan M. (1987) *Health and Illness – The Lay Perspective.* London: Tavistock Publications.

Campbell A (1984) *Moderated Love. A Theology of Professional Care.* London: SPCK.

Illitch I (1975) *Medical Nemesis.* Harmondsworth: Penguin.

Pearson A (1983) *The Clinical Nursing Unit.* London: Heinemann.

Pearson A (1987) *Primary Nursing.* London: Croom Helm.

White M (1987) *The Health Divide: Inequalities in Health in the 1980s. A Review.* London: Health Education Council.

Part II

5
Communication Network

This chapter is concerned with:

- Differentiating between personal and organisational communications
- Discussing some aspects of behaviour which can influence communication
- Discussing means by which organisational communication can be enhanced

It is widely acknowledged that good communications are essential to both the practice of nursing and the way in which it is managed. There are few of us who have not attended courses, workshops, or teaching sessions on this topic at some time or another in our careers, and it is certainly included as a separate subject in the majority of formal curricula, yet it remains a problem area. There is ample evidence to show that communication between nurses and patients is sometimes ineffective (Faulkner, 1980; Macleod Clark, 1983). Similarly at an organisational level, how often is the cry of 'nobody told me' heard, regardless of the plethora of papers and memos which arrive on our desks? So communication is a topic which must be raised and tackled in an effective way.

It can be suggested that good communications are the cornerstone of good practice. If information is misheard or misunderstood, it can lead to a myriad of problems for both patients and nurses. For example, at a clinical level, hints given by patients about their worries and fears can easily be missed, leading to unnecessary anxiety. At a more basic level, instructions about such things as changes in patients' medication may be misunderstood and lead to potentially dangerous mistakes. At an organisational level, information about proposed developments, changes in services provided by other departments such as catering or pharmacy, or the change of venue of meetings, can be missed, which inevitably leads to friction. Similarly, exchanges between nurses working in the same unit can be misheard or misinterpreted, particularly if se occur as veiled suggestions rather than through open discussion.

Suggestions made in many of the other chapters in this section are dependent on effective communication (e.g. performance review, introducing changes, assertiveness), but the purpose in this chapter is to introduce some basic ideas about communication to act as a starting-point for other work.

COMMUNICATION – WHAT IS IT?

Communication is the exchange of information between two or more people. Essentially, there are two different processes which need to be differentiated from one another, although some of the skills are common to both. Firstly there is communication at an interpersonal level – that is, messages passing directly between two or more people – and, secondly, there is communication at an organisational level where pathways have to be opened up in all directions in order that messages can pass between a large number of people. In either of these situations it is easy for the circuits through which messages flow to become blocked or broken and for the messages to get lost.

Attitudes, Behaviour and Communication

Attitudes can be described as settled ways of thinking about particular subjects and are very deep-rooted in all of us. Essentially, they arise out of what we believe to be right or wrong, good or bad, regardless of whether or not this is accurate. They are often formed very early in our lives, their development being dependent as much on social influences as on factual knowledge, and, once embedded, they are very difficult to change. Yet our attitudes to particular subjects can be very influential in the way we behave. It has been suggested (DHSS, 1983) that a chain of events can occur: what we believe to be true will influence our attitudes to a particular subject; in time this can influence our intentions, or proposed actions which, at the end of the day, affects the way we behave (Figure 5.1).

Belief → Attitudes → Intentions → Behaviour

Fig 5.1 A chain of events

Of course, the way in which we behave is a powerful means of communication; for example, some believe that all people should have equal access to health care and, as a consequence, that there should be no private beds in National Health Service hospitals. Such a belief can influence their attitudes towards private patients which, in this instance, may be negative. As a consequence, it may be that their intentions are to avoid this particular client group and so, in effect, they may receive less attention. Obviously, not everyone feels the same way about this particular topic but there are many other situations which can give rise to uncomfortable and negative feelings amongst nurses. It is sometimes worth making a little time to examine one's own feelings about particular things in order to see if one's attitudes do in fact influence the way in which one communicates with some people.

As far back as 1952, Peplau suggested that nurses should be able to manage their own behaviour in such a way as to act as a positive trigger to help patients and that, in order to be able to do this effectively, it is essential for nurses to become aware of their own feelings about some things which they may initially find distasteful, such as disfigurement, bad smells, dying or loss. Thus, the first step towards effective communication is self-awareness – an understanding of one's own feelings and self.

Burnard (1985) describes self-awareness as 'the gradual and continuous process of noticing and explaining aspects of the self, whether behavioural, psychological or physical, with the intention of developing personal and interpersonal understanding'. While there are some basic guides to communication which can be followed, these may well be ineffective if some time is not spent initially in knowing oneself a little better.

FIXED SETS

Moving into a conversation with a fixed view about the subject-matter can be a very effective block to communication for, if the conversation does not flow in the expected direction, the meaning can be lost. Alternatively, lack of attention to what is being said can occur, especially if this does not match expectations. This can be illustrated by the example of a nurse involved in a role-play, working with North West Spanner (a group of actors who play the part of patients in order to help health-care staff to develop communication skills). Once an interaction is completed, the actors stay 'in role' and give feedback of their responses and understanding, vividly displaying the situation.

The scene in question took place between the nurse and a patient who had just been transferred back to his home town, having been diagnosed as having lung cancer but not having learned of his condition. The nurse approached him with the firm idea that she would try to open up the opportunity for him to ask her what was wrong and, indeed, she displayed very good skills in this respect. Despite this, no such questions were asked and finally the conversation was ended with the idea of broaching the subject again at a later date.

During feedback, it became apparent that what this particular patient feared more than anything else was the pain which he associated with cancer. A brief passing comment had been made to his vision of cancer as something which 'eats away at your inside and causes terrible pain'. He was quite clear that, if he could have been reassured that this need not be the case, he would then have felt able to ask if, indeed, this was his diagnosis. Yet, because of the fixed ideas of the nurse prior to the interaction, the cues were missed.

While this example might seem extreme, it was very real and one of the most valuable learning experiences which the nurse went through. Such opportunities are not available to all, but maybe sharing her experiences will be of some help.

LISTENING

An awareness of the sort of things which can block listening may help nurses in their day-to-day practice, not only in the way they behave personally but also in 'setting the scene' to help patients hear what is being said. There are several factors which can affect listening, including the environment and the use of language.

The Environment

Many places in which nurses work are by no means ideal settings to facilitate good communication: they are often noisy, active places with many distractions. Noises which are often familiar to those who work regularly in the environment, and can therefore be interpreted readily, may well be very distracting to patients who may be unable to differentiate between sounds which are usual and those which may be a warning signal calling for attention. For instance, a change in someone's breathing pattern may be accepted by the nurses as 'normal' but may worry a patient who is unable to interpret the change.

While drawing curtains may reduce the number of visual distractions which can disrupt communication, it certainly does nothing towards cutting down the sounds. Sometimes, by reducing visual input, the noises can become even more difficult to interpret and hence cause greater worry. Furthermore, the fear of 'eavesdroppers' can be accentuated if people cannot see who is nearby and may be able to overhear what they are saying.

It is often not easy to find a quiet corner in which to talk, especially in hospital, yet there are ways round this difficulty. The ward office is an obvious answer but interruptions can occur. Some people have found the bathroom to be a good private spot, particularly if there is a lock on the door! Day rooms are not always fully used. Even going for a walk together, out of the ward, can be helpful.

If it is impossible to get away from a noisy, busy setting, recognising that what is familiar to the nurse may not be so to a patient can at least heighten awareness of potential distractions. Explaining some of the happenings may help to reduce the degree of invasiveness that these can give rise to.

Language

Simple words can often be interpreted by different people in different ways. Not only may they have different meanings but they may also awake different kinds of feelings according to people's past experiences. For example, the simple word 'dinner' may mean a mid-day meal, an evening meal or the main meal of the day. For some, it may be associated with a happy family event but for others a formal obligation. The use of jargon or abbreviations can also be confusing: how many times have we said to a patient, 'I'll do your "obs" in a minute'?, yet those who are unfamiliar with a clinical setting may have no notion of what this means.

Many words which we use frequently at work can certainly be open to misinterpretation. One patient gave a vivid description of her feelings when told she would need a simple mastectomy. To her, the word 'simple' implied that the procedure was unimportant and of little concern to those responsible for her treatment, and such an interpretation had caused her immeasurable distress. To the doctors it referred to a specific technical procedure. So the careful use of words is essential. Of course, we cannot always know what words may mean to others so a constant monitoring of what has been understood, rather than just what has been said, is essential.

EYE CONTACT

The importance of eye contact has been so widely discussed that it may seem redundant to talk about it further here. However, there are one or two points that are worth mentioning.

There is nothing worse than feeling as if someone is staring at you throughout a conversation, for it is neither natural nor comfortable to maintain eye contact at all times. Indeed, most people when they talk frequently look at different things, and regaining eye contact is one way of 'passing the conversation over' to indicate that it is the listener's turn to talk. However, as a listener, purposefully moving one's line of vision to another subject, such as a passing colleague, a distant telephone or a chart, is a very effective conversation stopper. At times it can be used as an intentional strategy, since the message of being either disinterested or too busy comes over loud and clear but, if the conversation is important as, for example, during assessment, it can be very distracting.

WRITTEN INFORMATION

It is well known that we are unable to recall a large proportion of what has been said to us and this is certainly made worse if the subject or surroundings are unfamiliar. There is now plentiful evidence that verbal information reinforced by written material is much more reliable and can, indeed, affect patients' lives.

One study has examined the use of written information for patients who have had below-knee walking plasters applied, with a significant improvement in their independence in fulfilling daily activities such as bathing or shopping (Pearson, 1987). The response of a group of patients who had written information about activities of living prior to discharge following surgery again showed very positive results (Vaughan, 1987).

The use of written information is a simple method of improving communication with patients. Reliance on memory alone can be risky, partly because the messages may be misheard but also because they may be forgotten. Of course, these principles apply equally well when considering communication between colleagues and the importance of the written word should never be under-estimated in ensuring that information does not get lost or distorted.

In this first section of the chapter, a few of the issues which can affect communication have been raised. Ample literature is available on this particular topic, some of which is listed at the end of the chapter, and it is strongly recommended that it be read.

ORGANISATIONAL COMMUNICATION

Any group of people who work together need to establish an effective communication system in order to avoid misunderstanding and to be able to work towards a common goal. Moreover, if the system of communication breaks down, all power and influence can be lost since, if messages do not get through effectively, the responses may not be as expected. So the establishment of a communication network which really works is essential to the smooth running of any organisation, whether small or large.

Within health care, there are many sub-groups working within the total organisation and channels have to be established at all levels and in all directions to ensure that messages are sent and received throughout it. For example, however good the senior clinical nurse is at sharing information with the rest of the clinical team, if she is unaware of, or has misinterpreted, information which may affect the total organisation, she cannot pass this on. Similarly, if accurate information is not passed through from a clinical to a managerial network, it cannot be expected that the information will be taken into account when organisational decisions are made, which can lead to significant difficulties at a later date.

A simple example may be the use of paper towels in hospital. As we all know, some paper towels are efficient at their purpose, while others absorb less well, flake and chafe the skin. Unless this message gets through to those who are responsible for arranging contracts with the suppliers, they cannot be blamed for making the wrong purchase. At a more significant level, if nurses do not supply managers with accurate information about the relationship between workload and workforce, their position is weakened when seeking resources.

As a starting point in establishing a good communication network, it is useful to work out the essential people or groups with whom one has to communicate. Figure 5.2 represents some of those people with whom a senior clinical nurse will need to make contact. Once they have all been identified, methods of maintaining effective two-way systems can be established.

Different approaches can be used for different groups, but what is important is that the method used should be known and understood by all concerned. Some ideas about methods of communication are given below: these are by no means exclusive and you may well have developed other systems.

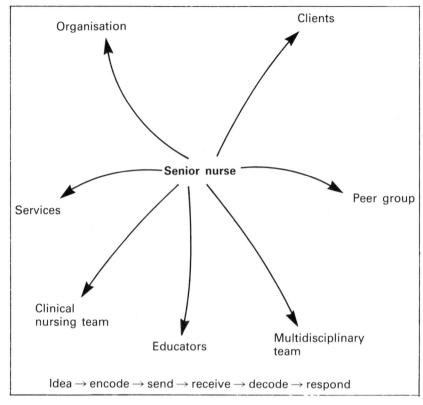

Fig 5.2 Lines of communication

MEETINGS

Many people throw up their hands in horror at the number of meetings they have to attend and they sometimes find that the time is not well spent. Yet a well run meeting is a very effective means of communication. There are, however, some basic ground rules which have to be followed if the meeting is to run well and these relate to:

- The purpose of the meeting
- Its membership
- Frequency and length
- An agenda
- Who takes the minutes
- Who will be responsible for action
- Who is to chair the meeting

The Purpose of the Meeting

It is very easy to waste time at meetings by confusing their purpose or functions so the first step in setting up a regular meeting is to decide exactly what its purpose is to be and what are legitimate items for discussion. At a clinical level, it is very important to differentiate between discussion of specific patients and their clinical care and the policy of the unit: thus, in a case conference the purpose would be to plan a care programme for a particular client, whereas the purpose of a business meeting may be to decide upon policies for the unit. If these two functions are not separated, it is highly likely that one will take precedence over the other, with a consequent imbalance between the two.

Meetings between doctors, paramedical staff and nurses can often be confused in this way. While it is common practice to have ward rounds or clinical conferences, it is less usual to see groups of health-care workers getting together specifically to discuss the policy of the unit in which they all work. Yet, if this is not agreed to by all members of the team, confusion can arise. Such a meeting does not have to take place in a formal setting around a conference table: indeed, in the unit office and over a cup of coffee may be a more appropriate setting. The important point is that time is set aside on a regular basis to ensure that policy issues are discussed.

Once the purpose of the meeting has been established, it is useful to make a short statement, in writing, about what it is so that it is clear to all those who attend. Furthermore, once the statement has been agreed by the members, it can be used as a means of controlling the content of the meeting that so, if inappropriate issues are raised at the wrong time they can be referred to the correct channels.

While this may sound a somewhat laborious task it is well worth the time and effort in the long run. Establishing a formal constitution for a meeting does not mean to say that the meeting itself has to be formal – it just ensures that the right topics are discussed by the right people at the right time.

Membership

The membership of a meeting obviously depends upon its purpose or function; for example, when it is a case conference it may be appropriate to involve the client and his or her relatives. At policy meetings about the clinical unit it is important that the senior members of each team should be represented, including the senior clinical nurse and the consultant. Members of the nursing team may choose to have separate meetings to discuss nursing policies, such as their philosophy, duty rotas or students' needs.

Frequency and Length of Meetings

On the whole, it is better to hold meetings at a set time and day on a regular basis, such as the last Wednesday of the month at 2 p.m. or every Tuesday at 10 a.m. If there is a very long interval between meetings, it is sometimes difficult for members to pick up the threads and important issues may also have got out of hand. Alternatively, meeting too frequently with no agenda items for discussion can be equally frustrating; the purpose of the meeting should give some idea of the frequency at which they should be held.

Some indication of the expected length of the meeting is also helpful as people are then aware of how much time they have to move through the agenda. They also need to know when they will be free to attend to other matters. While there is no hard and fast rule, short meetings at frequent intervals seem to work better than infrequent long ones. However, if the length of a meeting has been agreed, it does not mean that it has to be strictly adhered to: while it can be very annoying if meetings overrun, it is pointless to drag them out to the allotted time for the sake of appearance.

Agendas

Trying to hold a meeting without an agenda is like trying to find one's destination in unknown territory without a map. It is inefficient and time-wasting to expect people to attend without knowing what needs to be discussed. Whenever possible, agendas should be drawn up and circulated in advance so that those attending can give some thought to the subject beforehand. However, in some circumstances it may be that there is an agreed pattern to the meeting which can be followed on each occasion in a less structured manner.

The usual structure of an agenda is:

- Apologies for absence
- Minutes of the last meeting (to be agreed as correct or altered if necessary)
- Matters arising from minutes – where feedback is given or information updated
- New items – which have been notified in advance

- Any other business – giving the chance to raise issues which have not been included in the prepared agenda
- Confirmation of time, date and place of next meeting

Everyone who attends a meeting should have the opportunity to contribute to the agenda in order that all points of view can be covered, either formally through the preplanned agenda or under 'any other business'. Scanning the agenda before a meeting can give some idea of how much time there is for each topic, not forgetting the need to leave room for any other business which may arise.

Minutes

However informal the meeting, it is always worth while ensuring that the topics which have been discussed, and any conclusions which have been reached, are recorded. It is also useful to have a column down the side of the page where the name of the person who is to take action is included, thus making the responsibility clear. Hoping that someone will act without formally giving the responsibility to that person can lead to a diffuse situation where nothing gets done. Minutes can also be read by those who were unable to attend the meeting, thus ensuring that they are made aware of what was agreed and can contribute ideas to items still under discussion.

There is no need for minutes to be lengthy: in fact, they are far more likely to be read if brief and to the point. A master copy should always be kept in case members should lose their copies or the need arises to refer to matters that were dealt with at earlier meetings.

Chairperson

The function of the chairperson of a meeting is not to dominate the situation but to ensure that members keep to the point and that everyone who wishes to speak is given the opportunity. The chairperson need not be the most senior person present and in some instances the chair 'rotates' through the members.

While the procedure outlined above may seem rather onerous and formal, the basic principles should apply to any meeting which is held even if it is only a short gathering of, say, 20 minutes once a week. Certainly, if notes are not kept, information can easily get lost or not be passed on to those unable to attend.

WRITTEN COMMUNICATIONS

In any health-care setting, a constant flow of papers, the purpose of which is to pass on information, arrives on one's desk; however, it is not unusual for such papers to be filed in the waste bin before they reach their intended recipients. This situation can be remedied, at least in part, in several ways.

Firstly, a list of the names of those who should read the document can be attached to it, to be initialled and dated when read, and passed with the document to the next person; however, if a large number of people is involved this may be too time-consuming. Secondly, circulars can be pinned to a notice board but, again, it is worth attaching a list of those who may need the information so that it can be seen who has read them. However, beware of boring, out-of-date notice boards. If they are not well kept it is unlikely that people will continue to be motivated to read whatever information is displayed: this can be avoided by giving someone the responsibility for ensuring that the notice board is tidy and up to date.

Communications Books

Some units have a communications book where messages or comments can be left. Using this method, odd notes can be jotted down when they are first thought of rather than being left until a more formal occasion. They can also be used as a means of communicating pent-up feelings by those who find it difficult to talk about matters that are bothering them. Many nurses have found the use of a communications book to be an invaluable asset to their day-to-day practice.

The information recorded in the communications book can form the basis of the agenda for regular meetings of the unit nursing staff, although the items discussed still need to be included on the agenda. Once the comments have been dealt with they can be ticked or crossed through as a means of demonstrating that note of them has been taken and, where appropriate, acted upon.

In this chapter some ideas have been given about ways in which communication networks can be established in order to make sure that the right people have the right information at the right time. The subject is so broad that it has only been possible to raise a few topics which may be of value. Yet, effective communication is vital to us all if we wish to offer a service to patients which is both efficient and effective. Time spent on developing good communication skills and establishing effective systems is time well spent.

It is strongly recommended that attention be given to this subject since many of the other topics discussed in this book are dependent on the ability to be able to communicate effectively. Even though it may be uncomfortable to recognise that our communication skills are not as effective as they might be, it is worth while examining our own practice to see if there are ways in which it can be improved; it can be very rewarding if better mechanisms can be found. Paying some attention to how communication is effected is undoubtedly the foundation of good clinical practice.

EXERCISES

1. Is there a particular clinical topic or client group about which you consistently feel uncomfortable? Next time you find yourself in contact with someone in this situation, stop to think whether your feelings influence the way in which you behave.

2. Make a record of all the people with whom it is essential that you communicate, as shown on page 74. Now note the methods you use in each case to make sure that information can be passed between you and these people.

3. If, in Exercise 2, you felt that there may be more effective ways of communicating with one or more groups, work out a method which you think may be better and see whether it can be introduced to your practice.

4. If there are no records of discussions held between you and the people you work with about unit policies, discuss whether these could be introduced.

Further Reading

Argyle M (1983) *The Psychology of Interpersonal Behaviour.* Harmondsworth: Penguin.
Bridge W and Macleod Clark J (1981) *Communication in Nursing Care.* Chichester: HM+M/John Wiley and Sons.

Burnard P (1985) *Learning Human Skills.* London: Heinemann.
Continuing Nurse Education Programme (1986) *Interpersonal Learning (An Open Tech Project).* London and Manchester: Open Learning for Nurses.

6
A Unit Profile

This chapter aims to introduce you to:

- The purpose of a unit profile
- Some ideas about what may be included in a unit profile
- The way in which a unit philosophy can become a working document affecting day-to-day practice

A unit profile is a description of the various aspects of the work of a ward which can be used to inform nurses, other members of the health-care team, patients and their relatives; it may contain anything that can be justified as being informative and useful. Readers of this chapter may develop some of the ideas suggested here for their own units, but also create new ones which apply specifically to their own needs and circumstances. There is scope for you and your staff to be creative in producing a document which is interesting, enlightening, informative and personal to the unit.

A unit profile can be compared to a tourist guidebook. The guidebook is a resource which gives such diverse information as local customs and values, the best features of a place, how to use the amenities, interesting characters and colloquialisms. Such information is valued by visitors and residents, as well as by potential investors.

Similarly, the information contained in a unit profile can be of great importance to its users, who may include:

- Potential nursing applicants
- Anyone working or receiving care in the unit
- Managers supporting the unit work

This chapter explores the possible contents of a unit profile and discusses its uses for each of the groups of people identified above.

While still using the guidebook analogy, it is appropriate to point out that the quality of these books can vary: some are too long, some too short and some exaggerate the charms of the place – the last of these will expose the unit to hypercriticism by visitors whose expectations have been falsely raised. These attributes also apply to a unit profile which, if it represents the ideal rather than the reality, will not be well received once the truth is known.

THE CONTENTS AND FORMAT

The contents and format of a unit profile will depend on many things, including the purpose for which it is intended, the support given by other members of the multidisciplinary team, and the time available for its preparation. Careful consideration has to be given to the selection of essential elements for inclusion, and to the needs of the potential reader.

It is unlikely that work of this nature can be satisfactorily completed in haste and it will be found that time taken to plan will be well spent. The profile can be built up in sections; over time, more can be added and, when appropriate, out-of-date information removed. The work of drafting the profile can be distributed amongst the nursing staff, and it may also be thought desirable to include a section written by a patient, and by a doctor or another member of the multidisciplinary team.

One practical idea is to hold a master copy of the profile on the unit in a ring folder so that sections can be copied as required. For example, a new houseman will need sections on the nursing philosophy and work organisation, but will not require the parts explaining the off-duty rota or the ordering of stores. Of course, the doctor may have a particular interest in the off-duty rota, in which case he or she can refer to the master copy! In the same way, appropriate sections can be sent to nursing applicants or given to patients and their relatives.

Before beginning work on a section of the profile, the author will need to clarify its purpose with team colleagues and, to this end, it is logical and often helpful to provide written aims and objectives. Much time can be saved by ensuring that the expected content of each section of the profile is made known beforehand to all contributors in order to avoid overlapping and misunderstanding about what is required of them. Deadlines set for the completion of the work may solve the problem of unfinished masterpieces.

The Introduction

An introduction to the profile sets the scene and clarifies its purpose. It may also be necessary to explain the format of the document at this stage in order to make it easy to use. The writing style of the introduction can be very important since it can convey an image of the atmosphere on the unit. After reading the two examples given below it would be interesting to see which setting you would prefer to go to:

'This is an introduction to the policies and routines on this ward which must be read by all patients and doctors.'

'The nursing team hope that this description of the ward will be informative and help you to settle in as comfortably as possible.'

The following discussion identifies some of the items which may be included in a unit profile, although there is no hard-and-fast rule and at the end of the day the staff of each unit must decide for themselves what is most appropriate for them.

The Staff

An introduction to the staff of the unit can range from a simple list of names and positions to individual vignettes, which could include past work experience, what part of the country they come from, hobbies or interests. At first glance, the latter idea may not appeal, but try not to reject it without a little more consideration. A record of a nurse's past work experience can highlight her as a resource. For example, in an acute general ward to know that a particular nurse has ophthalmic experience could be useful if a blind patient is admitted, since she could act as consultant when planning care for that patient.

Short descriptions of interests and hobbies may act as a catalyst for stimulating conversations with patients who have similar interests. Indeed, we have no hesitation in asking patients about their interests and hobbies and recording them. However, it must be emphasised that this idea should not be pursued if staff do not feel comfortable with it: they may well be indignant, and rightly so, if anything is written about them without their consent.

Philosophy of Care: Developing a Framework for Practice

There are many different definitions of philosophy but, basically, to philosophise is to seek truth and wisdom thoughtfully and rationally. Philosophy is associated in many minds with argumentative academics, who ruminate in ivory towers or on river banks about things which are not really relevant to the real world. The idea of nurses taking time to philosophise in the hurlyburly, pragmatic health service today is seen by some as pretentious and time-wasting.

Yet we all philosophise to an extent, albeit over a bottle of red wine in the small hours discussing the meaning of life, or with colleagues after a shift, seeking to rationalise behaviour, and at times like these it is easier to give opinions, argue in an uninhibited way and listen to others. However, if the word philosophy is mentioned nurses often withdraw, not wishing to become involved, since they associate it with highbrow academics and unintelligible multisyllabic terminology – this need not be the case.

A unit philosophy is usually a concise statement of the nurses' attitudes, values and beliefs about issues which they consider important. If the word 'philosophy' is unacceptable, as it is to some, by all means call the exercise something different, perhaps a 'statement of beliefs'. However, whatever expression is chosen, the statements which are finally produced are fundamental to the manner in which the unit is run and the foundation of the conceptual framework for practice.

What we believe to be true, right or important has a fundamental effect on how we behave. A nurse who believes that nursing is about physical care and doing things for patients will behave in a different way from one who believes that it is about helping clients to care for themselves. A patient looked after by both these nurses may well become confused and dissatisfied with his inconsistent care; for example, one day he may be fed and the next, in his mind, 'abandoned' to feed himself.

Another example may be the nurse who believes that continuing education is important and worth while. This nurse is more likely to actively seek learning opportunities and support colleagues who wish to develop professionally. On the other hand, the nurse who does not value continuing education typically only attends study days if sent on them, and grumbles about the workload when others attend. When attendance at study days is monitored, patterns emerge which show clearly that some areas rarely send representatives. This may be a reflection of the underlying philosophy of the unit, as patient dependency and staffing levels were found by Burnip (1987) to be similar to those of units which are well represented.

Of course, nurses in a team cannot all be expected to have the same values and beliefs, since they will have developed and learnt in a variety of different social settings. Nevertheless, it is important that they should discuss their differences on fundamental issues which affect nursing practice, such as human dignity, individuality and rights. If differences result in antagonistic behaviour, the issue should then be re-explored and a consensus sought.

Before writing the unit philosophy, it is worth ensuring that all the nursing team understand the exercise and know that their contributions are important. The team then needs to decide on which issues they wish to make statements. Common choices are:

- The nature of people and human rights
- Methods of nursing
- Nursing goals
- Communication
- The nature of health
- Education

Once the issues have been decided, there are different methods of collecting together the general ideas and thoughts: three are described here, but there are other ways which may be preferred. Whatever means is chosen, the most important thing to remember is that, if people are to work within a philosophy, they must have had the opportunity to contribute to its development and feel that their contribution is both valued and respected.

A series of seminars attended by the unit staff can be held to discuss each issue in turn. The meetings are more effective if those attending come well prepared. They need to read and think about the topics to be discussed beforehand in order to be able to proffer constructive arguments. It is as well to select someone who is skilled in leading group discussions to run the seminar, since the group can easily wander from the topic under review. This may be an ideal opportunity to involve education staff.

At each meeting a statement may be agreed upon and, when the series is finished, they can be gathered together and reproduced as a draft document which can then be circulated to the members of the nursing team for consultation. The advantage of this method is that it ensures that all the nurses are involved and knowledgeable, but it has a practical difficulty, namely the time it takes to organise and hold meetings at the same time as running a unit.

Occasionally, opportunities arise such as closure for decorating or repairs which offer an ideal opportunity to get all the staff together. Some units have chosen to meet in the evenings for a short while to try to achieve their aims; others have found that meeting for a short period after the lunchtime handover has suited their needs.

The second approach is to set up concurrent sub-committees to investigate each issue, which then report back at one grand meeting, probably in the evening to ensure maximum attendance. The provision of food and drink may help the flow of thought!

A final method which has been successful in some units is to ask each person to contribute his or her views on the agreed topics in writing. If people are worried initially about making their views public, their contributions can be placed anonymously in an 'ideas box' (this also takes the pressure off those who do not wish to contribute at this stage). Once the ideas have all been presented, one person can collate them into a series of statements which can then be discussed at a meeting of the whole team, as described above.

It is recognised that all these ways do take a little extra time but, in the end, the use to which philosophy can be put makes it all worth while.

Besides circulating the final copy to all members of the nursing team, meetings need to be held to discuss the extent to which nursing behaviours match the philosophy. For example, take the statement, commonly written in philosophies, 'We believe in the holistic nature of people'. We all need to ask what evidence there is in our practice to show that this is really what we believe.

It may be decided to make the philosophy a regular agenda item at the unit meetings and, of course, it is to be hoped that the subject will be discussed informally. There is a danger if this is not done that the philosophy, although full of 'good stuff', is not connected with or reflected in practice.

Figure 6.1 is an example of the way in which what we believe in or value can affect day-to-day practice. None of the statements is right or wrong but simply a comment on the subject concerned. Two opposing views are given intentionally to show the extremes that exist.

Because we nurse in a pragmatic rather than an ideal system, there are likely to be some inconsistencies between the philosophy and practice. Schein (1969) describes three states concerned with beliefs and action which people may pass through, some of which are more comfortable to live with than others. These stages are:

1. *Dynamic stability*   He describes this as a stage in which people match their beliefs, values and attitudes to practice. There is no conflict.

2. *Precarious Stability*   This is a state in which people know that their practice does not match their beliefs. However, they are responding by making some changes in either practice or in their beliefs (the latter is a difficult process). This stage of precarious stability is well known to the majority of us, and it is a state, Schein suggests, which requires a great deal of energy. Ways of coping with this extra demand should be planned and some ideas

Statement	Effect on Practice
People	
1. Are biological creatures subject to disease	Assessment will only be concerned with biological functions and disease
2. Are holistic beings who function as a whole	Assessment will include social and psychological aspects
3. Should take the advice of experts	Patients/clients should be told what is the right course of action
4. Have a right to choose	Patients/clients are given sufficient information to choose alternative approaches to treatment (if they wish)
Health	
1. Is the absence of disease	Cure at all costs
2. Is feeling well and able to achieve those things which are important to the individual	Establish individual's desired level of 'wellness' which may/may not conform to health workers' view of health
Nursing	
1. Is caring for people	Nurses will provide care (do *for*)
2. Is helping people to care for themselves	Nurses will help people (when they can or wish) to care for themselves (do *with*)
3. Is primarily concerned with the patient as an individual	Will view the patient's family as a secondary concern (who have temporarily handed over care to nurses)
4. Is concerned with the patient as an individual who is part of a family and society at large	Will be concerned about how the family is affected by the patient's hospitalisation and help them (if they wish) to contribute to care

Figure 6.1 The influence of philosophy on practice. (After Vaughan, 1986)

are offered in Chapter 10 which may be helpful in finding that extra bit of energy.

3. *Instability* Schein describes this as a state in which the behaviour of people does not match their beliefs and no change is planned or made. An example of this state may be that a staff nurse believes in professional nursing where the registered nurse takes responsibility for helping a number of patients within a holistic framework but, in practice, the senior nurse insists on having sole contact with all relatives. This is a very uncomfortable situation which will not be tolerated for long: the staff nurse will either leave, or stifle her beliefs.

Although Schein was writing about the theory of change, his ideas are also applicable to the situation where a new unit philosophy has been prepared. If one thinks about it, it may be agreed that few nurses are in a state of dynamic stability, the majority being in the state of precarious stability. Writing and using a philosophy is unlikely to be a cosy self-congratulatory exercise, but one which entails a great deal of soul-searching and will probably result in changes being made. It is as well to be aware of this before embarking on the exercise.

What happens to the final document is crucial. It can either become an item of passing interest kept in the office desk drawer or it can become a working philosophy – one that affects practice and changes over time. If the former occurs, much of the time which has been spent in preparing it is lost, so it is important that the unit philosophy should be a 'living' item, which is easily accessible, often discussed, reviewed at regular intervals and the guiding light behind the development of practice.

Staff Development Progamme

This may be simply a factual description of the opportunities for professional development. An analysis of the various resources is one way to begin, and some of the things which are widely available may include:

- The library
- Learning packs
- Journals received on the ward
- Study rooms which may be used by unit staff
- People with specialist knowledge

Brief resumés of courses and workshops available within the district, and how to apply for them, are frequently made available by the continuing education department of the school of nursing, or sometimes by the district nursing office. Nurses may well be disappointed if it is intimated that they can attend anything that interests them, since this may not always be possible.

It may be a good idea to explain how attendance is fairly distributed amongst the nurses and for the knowledge gained through attendance at workshops, conferences and study days shared with the rest of the team. In some units, there is an expectation that a written report will be submitted after attending a conference; others have a less formal approach but, nevertheless, expect feedback from those who attend.

If there are schemes such as a journal club, careers advice, learning contracts and so forth within the unit they should be included in the profile. Credibility can be added to the document if a report of the learning activities completed in the previous six or twelve months is included.

Learning Opportunities for Students

Students may appreciate information such as the times when the clinical teacher is available and where messages can be left for her. Copies of the course curricula may be of value, as well as clarification of the learning objectives for this experience. Special opportunities which the clinical experience may offer may be itemised, and details of the mentor system, if it is being used, can be given, thus ensuring that students know who to refer to if they have difficulties or queries and who will be responsible for monitoring their progress.

It may also be appropriate to refer students to the section on professional development and invite them to join the qualified staff whenever they feel it would be helpful. They may well gain by reading projects and papers written by the experienced clinical nurses.

The students' attention can also be drawn to particular learning opportunities in the unit, such as a colleague who has particular expertise in counselling or the opportunity for visits to the cardiac catheter theatre. An explanation of the protocol for arranging individual learning experiences may also help the student; for example, does she have to make arrangements personally or will the ward staff arrange a rotation with other learners?

Information for Patients

It might be worth considering asking a group of patients to write this section. However, if this idea does not appeal, an alternative could be to ask a number of patients what written information they would have liked to have been given on first being admitted to the unit. Some suggestions might include:

- A diagram of the ward
  and details of
- Visiting times and meal times
- Making and receiving telephone calls

- Times of the newspaper rounds
- Times of doctors' rounds
- Nurses, uniforms
- How to make complaints

Some hospitals send a booklet to patients before admission and, in order to avoid duplication, it is worth checking on the contents so that time and effort may be saved.

Once the profile is in use, patients may well add to this section information which they think others may wish to have.

The Unit Objectives

However well-run the unit, there is always something else to strive for as new ideas emerge or new learning takes place. Identifying objectives which will be aimed for jointly can be both an effective means of communication and a motivator to remind the staff of their plans. These objectives are set either annually or at six-monthly intervals and state the new work to be achieved by the team. Examples might be that, by the end of the year:

- A performance review system will have been introduced. Each nurse will have agreed standards of performance and will have had one review interview (see Chapter 7)
- The number of study days taken by staff will increase by 2 per cent
- A mentor system for students will be started

At the end of the year a report and evaluation of these activities could be added to the objectives section.

The number of sections which can be included in a ward profile is considerable, but there are no hard-and-fast rules about what should or should not be present. The ideas given above are just a few which may be of help as a starting point. Other sections can include inventories of equipment, the organisation of nursing work, the ordering of stores, a précis of the nursing model used for practice, and many more ideas. However, the final document will be unique to the setting for which it has been prepared and it would be inappropriate to describe a set pattern; it is for this reason that no example of a profile has been given here.

THE USES OF A UNIT PROFILE

The New Nurse

Choosing to work in a new area can be a formidable experience. Sometimes new nurses are upset because practice is not what they expected or were used to in their previous post. This type of misunderstanding can be offset to some extent by an informal visit (which can be costly for the applicant) and probing questions at interview. However, these strategies do not substitute for a written commitment from the unit which can enhance the potential applicant's understanding prior to appointment and avoid a potential mismatch.

In turn, the nurse who has read the unit profile and disagrees with any aspect of it is at liberty to withdraw her application, saving time for all concerned. For example, she may not like the idea of primary nursing; if, however, she proceeds with her application it can be inferred that she intends to work within the system and not obstruct it.

The unit profile is a marketing asset and should be exploited to the full. The nurse who receives a profile with an application form may well be impressed and choose to apply to that unit rather than another. However, be warned again not to exaggerate the information it contains as this tactic may attract staff but certainly will not help to keep them.

The Clients

Factual information in the profile might help patients to settle comfortably in a hospital ward or be conversant with the community services available, especially as verbal information is not always complete or remembered. It might be the case that patients still expect clinical units to be places that are regimented and rule-laden; in strange surroundings they need permission to do many things they would normally do without thinking at home, for example taking a bath in the evening.

Relatives sometimes have the same concern and fears, which can be very inhibitive and make them feel worried and unwelcome. The profile is not a substitute for conversation between the nurse, the patient and relatives – it is a back-up. However, the provision of written information for patients is one small way of making life a little less stressful. It can act as a useful reference point, an aide memoire and a guide to what can be expected.

The Nursing Team

Besides being a useful record of resources, beliefs and activities, the unit profile can also be used to evaluate some aspects of the team's work: either they are providing the service the profile suggests, or they are not. Individuals can measure the part they are contributing to the whole.

The profile can help communication and clarify relationships with the multidisciplinary team since the contribution which the nurses can make will be made clear. If others, such as doctors, physiotherapists, social workers and so forth, can see what the nurses are hoping to achieve, working relationships will then become clear. In turn, other team members may choose to add to the profile so that a whole picture of the provision available within the unit is included.

Management

Managers appreciate units which can clearly define the work that they do and how well they do it, and state their objectives for the next year. When bidding for extra resources it is much easier to present a convincing case when this type of information is to hand, especially in these days of economic constraint, accountability and general management.

The unit profile is a management tool and a useful adjunct to communication. It must be remembered, though, that it will only be as good as the people who make it, the practice it reflects and the manner in which it is used. It will not camouflage a poor unit for very long but is something which those who are striving for excellence may be proud of.

EXERCISES

1. Make a list of the sections you would include in a ward profile for your particular area. Arrange them in order of priority.

2. Introduce the concept of ward profiles to your staff at the next ward meeting. Discuss the advantages with them.

3. Write an action plan for making a ward profile, stating who will do what, and when.

Further Reading

Campbell A (1984) *Moderated Love. A Theology of Professional Care.* London: SPCK.

Pearson A (1987) *Primary Nursing.* London: Croom Helm.

Styles M (1982) *On Nursing – Towards a New Endowment.* St Louis: C V Mosby.

Wright S (1986) *Building and Using a Model of Nursing.* London: Heinemann.

7
Performance Planning and Review

This chapter aims to:

- Discuss the positive aspects of performance planning and review
- Help the reader to prepare a standards of performance document to be used for performance review
- Estimate the amount of time this system will take to set up and run

The purpose of this chapter is to describe a logical sequence of steps that will lead to positive performance planning and review.

In too many instances in the past, performance appraisal has been imposed upon nurses and poorly executed, which has served to give it a bad name. Most readers will be able to recall instances where the use of appraisal has seemed to be of little value. Indeed, some have suggested that it is time-wasting, punitive and sometimes destructive. With the new title 'performance planning and review' it is hoped to shake off the negative attitudes towards the old-style appraisal system. The new title conjures up the impression of a process which is deliberate, positive and controlled. Most of the effort in this process is expended when setting the system up rather than in mopping up after the deed, as with the old system; in other words, it represents proactive rather than reactive management.

When accurate information is not available, staff have to rely on their self-esteem fed by sporadic praise or reproof from senior nurses, patients, relatives and colleagues. Some nurses continue present practice simply because 'nothing disastrous has happened yet'. Worse still are examples of nurses who have failed to make the grade and leave with platitudes such as 'hard and willing worker' or 'all the patients love her' ringing in their ears. Unfortunately, a capacity for hard work and popularity are not the principal criteria for success in nursing.

Regular performance appraisal interviews alone are not the answer. To discuss how well someone is doing, before telling her how well she is expected to perform, is putting the cart before the horse. If performance review is to be beneficial to the manager, her staff and the organisation as a whole, considerable thought and planning must be applied to it.

Most people crave honest accurate information about their performance at work. If staff know precisely what is expected of them they can monitor their own performance. Having objectives to work towards allows the performer to make choices, the mental part of work described by Brown and Jacques (1965) as 'exercise of discretion'. This ability to make choices within a defined area of responsibility makes work interesting. Regular feedback of progress either gives workers the confidence to continue and improve or serves as an early warning for them to seek help in specific areas.

THE PURPOSE OF PERFORMANCE PLANNING AND REVIEW

Before embarking on this project, the reviewer needs to identify clearly the purpose and nature of the exercise and to perceive it as being important. To carry out performance appraisal merely because of an edict from on high is to reduce it to a bureaucratic chore. There are many benefits to be gained for those who plan and review staff performance but they should be wary of clouding the issue with multiple objectives. The prime benefit to be gained is the individual's improved performance in the current job. Spin-offs such as improved relationships, communication, identification of promotion prospects and so forth (Philp, 1983), although welcome, may each require individual attention and the use of different tactics.

PERFORMANCE PLANNING

Reviewers who have not clarified their own work will find it more difficult to do so for subordinates. Boundaries between the two may cross, causing confusion and problems associated with shared responsibility. There could, for example, be confusion between a sister and primary nurse in relation to prescribing patient care if their roles and responsibilities are not clear. So the first step must be to be clear about one's own work role and the way in which it will be fulfilled.

Once this step has been taken the performance reviewer and members of the team need to be able to define together:

- The aim of their job
- The key result areas
- The performance standards expected

The Aim of the Job

Aims clarify direction and purpose and are statements of the reason for working. They are broad statements which identify areas of work upon which individuals should concentrate their efforts. The first question to be asked when moving towards performance review is, 'What is it that the individual ultimately aims to achieve at work?' This can be a very simple statement such as:

'To provide safe nursing care to all patients and their families.'

'To manage and supervise care givers in order to facilitate safe nursing care for patients and their families.'

It is essential that the reviewer and the worker agree upon what the main aim of work is to be if they hope to agree on its content. Any job description should include a statement of the aim, and most employees will have seen and accepted this before appointment. However, difficulties do sometimes arise because some people:

- Do not have a job description
- Have no recollection of their job description
- Do not refer to it
- Have an inadequate or outdated job description

Any of these problems should be sorted out before going further, since misunderstanding at this stage can only lead to confusion. For example, a nursing auxiliary may perceive that the aim of her work is to 'keep all the patients clean and comfortable at all times'. Her supervising nurse may perceive that the aim of her work is to 'give care to patients according to qualified nurses' instructions'. Inevitably, the work this nursing auxiliary does and what is expected of her will differ, yet she cannot be blamed if the major aim of her work was not made clear in the first place.

Key Result Areas

Key result areas should also be made clear in the job description. They identify parts of work that directly contribute to the overall aim of the job. For a primary nurse or senior clinical nurse, key result areas are commonly divided into management, practice and teaching/learning components. Examples of key result areas for a primary nurse may include:

Teaching/learning

- Teaching and supervising learner nurses
- Helping patients to learn to care for their own health
- Evidence of continuing professional development

Practice

- Making written prescriptions of care for a named group of patients
- Carrying out the care prescribed for his or her own group of patients or another nurse's when acting as an associate nurse
- Making written evaluations of care given
- Contributing towards the maintenance of a cohesive ward team

Management

- Ensuring the safety of patients and staff on the ward
- Liaising with members of the multidisciplinary team

These are only examples of some key result areas and are not presented as a comprehensive job description; however, they do demonstrate the sort of content one would be looking for in key result areas.

Although statements such as those given above are a useful guide in performance review, they are still not precise enough to be useful when objectively considering work performance because they leave room for different perceptions which can lead to confusion. For example, the reviewer's and the primary nurse's ideas of what teaching and supervising learner nurses entails may be quite different. So there is further step to be undertaken in preparing for performance review, namely setting standards of performance.

STANDARDS OF PERFORMANCE

A standard is a measure, in this case a measure against which performance can be compared. Nursing is not an easy phenomenon to measure; however, measurement is possible and is made easier if it is broken down into the following steps described by Bloch (1977).

Identifying Criteria

For each of the key result areas, decide upon the criteria which could indicate that the particular responsibility was being met. For example:

Key result area
Contributing towards a
cohesive ward team

Criterion
Attendance at and participation
in ward meetings

Method of Measurement

The next step is to decide upon the method of measurement; in this case the number of meetings attended and number of items put forward for the agenda might be reasonable.

Method of measurement
Number of meetings attended
Number of agenda items proposed

Standards

The standard is the desired level to be achieved and it must be realistic. In some instances, one can include the percentage or frequency with which the criterion should be maintained, thus recognising and allowing for those times when it would be unrealistic to expect it to be met. Initially, the level set may be arbitrary. The clinical team will need to discuss and decide on a level which is reasonable in the light of past experience and knowledge of local structural constraints, such as staffing levels and shift patterns.

Standard
At least one meeting per month
At least two agenda items in six months

Norms

In time, a norm will be evident – that is, the usual type of behaviour for the setting. In the light of experience it may be appropriate to alter the standard to a more realistic level. We often overestimate when first embarking on identification of standards but sometimes may not be optimistic enough. For example, if the staff are attending three meetings a month on average, it would be reasonable to change the *minimum* standard to two meetings per month.

It is much easier to construct standards in a group, as the ideas seem to snowball. Furthermore, if nurses have been involved in writing standards for their own work, they are more likely to be acceptable and achievable. These are two of the criteria described by Philp (1983) as being essential when setting standards.

The other criterion Philp named is validity – in other words, is what is being measured worth measuring; does it demonstrate actions contributing to the key result area? For example, it would be possible to set a standard such as 'All patient assessments should be written in blue ink.' This may look attractive but hardly demonstrates that the nurse has an accurate assessment on which to base her prescription of care. An example of a standards of performance document for one component of a primary nurse's role is shown in Figure 7.1.

Once the standards have been identified, a draft standards document can be prepared and circulated to all those involved for consultation. All comments should be agreed and amendments made if necessary. The amount of leeway in each standard

Primary Nurse	Achieved Signature	Date
Prescription of nursing care All new patients assigned to the primary nurse will have a written nursing assessment within 24 hours, 90 per cent of the time.		
Care plans that are clearly written, and agreed by the patient, will be available for use by the patients and associate nurses within 4 hours of the nursing assessment, 90 per cent of the time.		
Care plans will be updated on each day that the primary nurse is on duty.		
A written evaluation of the care given to a patient will be made on each day that the primary nurse is on duty, 90 per cent of the time.		
Nursing care Patients will receive all prescribed care from their primary nurse on at least 3 days in a week.		

Figure 7.1 Standards of performance document

statement will depend on the role of the person for whom it is intended. Thus, if the document is being prepared for an unqualified member of the team, the prescription will be very tight and detailed, whereas a qualified team member is in a position to exercise a much greater degree of discretion within an overall framework.

It is also important to avoid the trap of writing too many standards for each key result area because they then become restrictive and stifle individuality and creativity by pedantically prescribing every nursing action.

Once the standards document is prepared and available to the relevant staff, most of the work has been done. Staff now know the purpose of their jobs, what their responsibilities are and how well they are expected to perform. They also know what contribution other members of the team are supposed to make. We have all worked with people who spent a disproportionate amount of time doing something they were particularly good at or liked doing, such as teaching, while the rest of us got on with all the work! This can be both frustrating and the cause of friction in a team. Yet, unless expectations are made clear in the first place, it is understandable that such situations will occur, reaffirming the need to clarify the boundaries of a work role and make clear the standards which are expected.

PERFORMANCE REVIEW

Individual Meetings or Interviews

Once performance standards have been identified, it is relatively easy to proceed to individual performance review. It is at this stage that each nurse has the opportunity to spend time at meetings with her manager which are devoted specifically to her own work and future plans.

There are three types of meeting or interview that may be arranged in the course of performance planning and reviewing:

- Preliminary
- Intervening
- Review and planning

It is not within the remit of this chapter to discuss the art of interviewing. However, it is worth remembering that attention should be paid to practical details such as a suitable venue, length of interview, comfort, and choice of appointment time to fit in with the commitments of both interviewee and interviewer. The use of communication skills to encourage the interviewee to talk, and active listening to demonstrate that what is communicated is heard and valued, are essential skills within performance review.

Preliminary Meeting

The preliminary meeting is an essential start to a review of performance and, ideally, should take place between one and three months after employment has begun. (The new employee should be given a sufficient period of time in which to settle in and find her feet but this should not be so long that she feels neglected.) It is an occasion when the nurse and her manager sit down together and agree what work is to be done in the following months, and it also offers them both a useful opportunity to get to know each other better. No comment about the nurse's performance should be made at this stage; such an approach would be unfair because she has no prior knowledge of the standards required except those included in the job description.

Before coming to the meeting the nurse should be told what its purpose is and be conversant with the standards of performance document for her grade. During the meeting the following topics may be covered:

- Agreement on standards of performance
- Identification of any potential problems
- Formulation of plans for the nurse's development
- Discussion of the form of the next meeting
- Agreement on a date for the next meeting
- Identification of sources of help for the nurse, if required before the next meeting

It may be possible for the nurse or the manager to foresee potential problems with any of the standards. A plan to overcome such problems may then be drawn up with clear descriptions of the contributions to be made by the nurse and manager. An example of an action plan of this kind is shown in Figure 7.2.

A record of the date and time of the meeting should be made, and a copy of the standards of performance and plan, if there is one, should be kept in the nurse's file. It is essential that she should have access to this for reference, or otherwise have her own copy.

The preliminary meeting is a one-off affair. When the system is introduced, all staff will need to have the opportunity for a preliminary interview, but after this initial effort only new staff will need to be seen, soon after they have completed their orientation programme. The interval between the preliminary

| Problem | Standard | Plan | | Review Date |
		Nurse	Manager	
Dislikes public speaking and has difficulty in writing reports due to inexperience	Will share information gained on study days with ward team by presenting it at the next meeting. Will write a report	Will listen to talk given by S/N May 3/7	Will listen to talk and spend 15 min. discussing it with nurse	3/7
		Will attend a study day with S/N May 21/7	Will arrange off duty and expenses	2/7
		Will prepare a written report with S/N May and join in a discussion group	Will help to plan the written report and give constructive comments	24/7
				10/8

Signature .... Date ....

Signature .... Date ....

Evaluation

Comments

Signature .... Date ....

Signature .... Date ....

Figure 7.2 Action plan

meeting and the review and planning meeting is arbitrary. Three months would be reasonable, in most cases, to allow the nurse to settle in and test the standards, but some nurses who feel insecure in a new role may request a meeting at an earlier date whilst an experienced nurse may find a six-month gap appropriate.

Intervening Meeting

An intervening meeting is arranged when a nurse consistently fails to meet standards and it is hoped that it would seldom be needed. It may be initiated by either the nurse or her manager and should be arranged as soon as possible after awareness of the need since the nurse may be feeling stressed. It should be emphasised that this is not a disciplinary meeting, but is necessary to investigate the reasons why the nurse is unable to meet standards. Most of us need help at some stage in our careers.

The nurse should be given time to think and explain her difficulties. It seldom helps if managers jump in with their interpretation as this gives the impression that their minds are already made up. The reasons for poor performance are multiple (Stewart, 1981), but clarifying them will guide both the nurse's and the manager's choice of a solution. If it is appropriate for the nurse to continue with her present responsibilities, an action contract should then be drawn up in the same way as shown in Figure 7.2, with plans to help the nurse to achieve the standard within a certain time. If the nurse is unwell or particularly stressed, it may be appropriate to reduce her responsibilities for a specific amount of time while she receives help and regains her strength.

Nurses who do not fulfil their part of the contract and continue to underperform may be warned, and later disciplined. In these instances, records of meetings, standards of performance, action contracts and evaluations are useful.

Performance Review and Planning Meeting

At this meeting, performance is compared with standards and the nurse is invited to identify any problems and is complimented on achievements. If standards have been achieved, there is no need to spend much time in retrospection. Problems are dealt with in the same way as at the other two meetings.

If the nurse keeps the same role, new targets, maybe a little above the basic standards, will need to be stated. As a nurse becomes more experienced in a role it may, in some instances, be appropriate to expect a little more of her; for example, after one year as a primary nurse her case-load may be increased. Any adjustments must be agreed and fair and it is worth bearing in mind that there is a risk that good performers may be overloaded. While the old saying, 'If you want a job done give it to a busy person' may ring true, there is a limit to what can reasonably be expected from any one individual.

Nurses who have achieved the required performance standards can then look forward. Bearing in mind their career aspirations, they are in a position to state work objectives for the coming six or twelve months. They may wish to gain more managerial experience, or start formal teaching. This is the time for nurses to express their talents and creative abilities. Once objectives are written, appropriate plans can be formulated, the manager agreeing on how much support she is able to give the nurse in terms of time, expertise and experience, bearing in mind the needs of the unit and other staff.

It should be remembered that a high turnover of staff is a reality in many areas of nursing and that changing jobs is often desirable early in a career in order to broaden experience and consolidate learning in different areas. Thus, nurses should be able to discuss with their managers, without fear, any plans that they may have to make a move. Similarly, personal wishes, such as the desire to start a family, can be accommodated within the plans, giving consideration to experience which may smooth the path to coming back to work after maternity leave.

Plans may be made for keeping in touch while the nurse is away from practice, such as some teaching input to the bank nurse education programme, or working through one of the distance learning packages. In this way both confidence and an interest in nursing can be maintained and improve the chances of part-time employment at a later date which would benefit both the individual concerned and the organisation, particularly in the light of the apparent shortage of qualified staff in some areas.

The date of the next performance review and planning meeting also needs to be discussed; again, this is arbitrary but any date between six months and a year ahead seems usual. On the whole, staff should all have the same amount of time between meetings since erratic timings lead to speculation on performance, with comments such as, 'I can't be as good as you if she wants to see me every five months' being made.

Records of the date and time of the meeting, standard achievement (a tick beside the standard is all that is required) and forward planning should be kept in the nurse's file. A signature is required in order to show that there is agreement on the standards of performance to be worked towards over the following months.

Once this cycle has been put in motion it should be quite easy to keep up the momentum. If staff find it useful, and our experience shows that they do, they will support the system and look forward to each meeting. Although it is recognised that a system of this kind takes some time to establish, at the end of the day the time is well spent since it can lead to a happy working team who know both what is expected of them and how well they are doing.

This is not the only system of performance review, and readers are encouraged to investigate the subject more closely before choosing one which suits their particular circumstances. However, it is widely used in American hospitals and in general management in this country and many believe that it is a good choice for those who are optimists, who believe in McGregor's 'Y' theory that people want to work and will grow and develop in the right circumstances. This type of system supports staff by clearly stating what they must do and then encouraging them to develop beyond the minimum standards required (Figure 7.3).

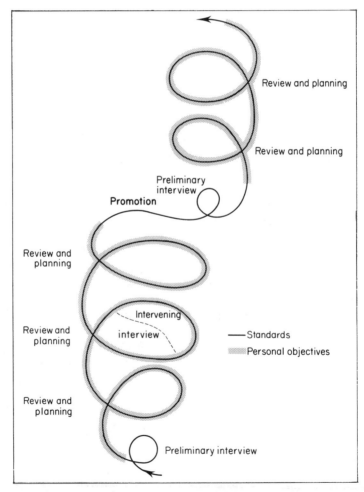

Fig 7.3 Ongoing performance review

EXERCISES

1. Take your own job description and write some standards for the key result areas.

2. Prepare, with the use of more material, a talk for your staff introducing the concept of performance planning and review. Critically discuss it with them.

3. Negotiate with your staff to come to an agreement about a phased introduction of performance review within an agreed length of time and then . . . action the plan!

Further Reading

Philp T (1983) *Making Performance Appraisal Work*. Maidenhead: McGraw-Hill.

Stewart V and Stewart A (1981) *Managing the Poor Performer*. Aldershot: Gower.

Video Arts (1985) *The Unorganised Manager. Parts 3/4*. Watford: Video Arts Ltd.

8
Professional Education

The purpose of this chapter is to:

- Outline current views on the educational process
- Discuss how these may affect nurse education
- Look at ways in which continuing education for nurses may be facilitated
- Discuss the need and responsibility for continuing education

Education was identified in Part I of this book as being one of the aspects of nursing which has been greatly affected by the changes which have been, and still are, taking place. In order to meet the challenge of change, nurses must have access to an educational programme which will facilitate the personal and professional development necessary to fulfil the changing role.

Many reports have been commissioned which have outlined proposals for change in educational philosophy and structure. The most recent is Project 2000 (UKCC, 1986), commissioned by the United Kingdom Central Council for Nurses, Midwives and Health Visitors. This report outlines proposals in relation to:

- The role of the future nurse practitioner
- Preparation for registration involving core and branch programmes
- Competences required for registration
- Specialist qualifications
- Student status
- Discontinuation of enrolled nurse training

The report points out that, although the programmes of education described in detail are only concerned with bringing the student to the point of registration, it is also essential that the registered practitioner must have opportunities for consolidation and then for continued updating of knowledge and skills. The need for continued updating is supported by Jacobi (1976) who reminds us that knowledge can be out of date in as little as five to eight years. Project 2000 goes on to say that there should also be opportunities for further development in specialist fields, which include clinical specialities, teaching, management and research, and suggests that this can be achieved through courses which will lead to a recognised qualification.

The purpose of this chapter is to consider the continuing education of the qualified nurse by reviewing the following:

- The need for continuing education
- The nature of education
- The learning processes and resources

THE NEED FOR CONTINUING EDUCATION

As stated in Chapter 1, change is an integral part of living, and inherent in any change are the processes of adjustment and adaptation. However, in order to ensure that positive adjustment or adaptation will occur, we may be required deliberately to acquire new skills, knowledge, and attitudes. Therefore, continued, planned learning is essential if the nurse practitioner is to meet the challenge of change and thus the needs of the society he or she serves.

The Code of Professional Conduct (UKCC, 1984) clearly identifies the professional duty of the nurse in terms of both maintaining and improving professional knowledge and competence. Surely this can only be achieved through continuing education? Project 2000 points out that the registered practitioners require ongoing development in order that they may firstly consolidate their role and then expand into the specialist practitioner, teaching or managerial roles. This, again, can only be achieved through continuing education.

A discussion paper has recently been released by the UKCC (1987) relating to mandatory, periodic refreshment for nurses and health visitors. If, or when, mandatory, periodic refreshment becomes a reality, continuing education will not only be a need but will also be an essential requirement to enable all practitioners to continue to practise.

However, a word of caution may be given in relation to mandatory refresher courses. It is very easy to fall into the trap of attending courses for the sake of it or just to fulfil requirements rather than because the courses meet the learning needs of the individual. So, while the importance of such a step is not denied, care must be taken that good use is made of the opportunity.

THE NATURE OF EDUCATION

Nursing is moving from an occupation with an associated training period to that of a profession where its members are considered to be educated in such a way as to offer a specific service to the public. Although the debate regarding occupation versus profession and training versus education is not considered here, it is necessary in the light of change to clarify thoughts and ideas about education in the context of the continuing education of nurses.

Peters (1966) associates education with learning. Jarvis (1983), however, points out that education is not just learning; he relates it to learning in terms of the educational process, this being a course of action or a series of events in which learning is intended. Therefore, only intended learning is considered in the discussion of education, although it is recognised that learning can also happen unintentionally as an everyday experience.

The notion of planned or intended learning requires further clarification as it may be considered legitimate to learn by indoctrination and without understanding. From the writings of Dewey (1916), Hare (1964) and Peters (1966), Jarvis (1983) concludes that education is any planned series of incidents, having a humanistic basis, directed towards the participants' learning and understanding. If nurses are to participate in educational processes and continue to do so throughout their professional careers, there are implications for all of us in the above statement in terms of value systems, beliefs, learning strategies, and status of the learner.

The use of the term 'continuing education' is also a product of the professionalisation of nursing, with continuing education replacing the familiar postbasic in-service training. The view that education is a continuing process is inherent in the description by Davies (1976) who describes it as being a lifelong process which helps people to develop personally, socially and professionally. If education is to be considered in terms of a lifelong process, there is perhaps a need to review learning in relationship to the adult learner who is central to the discussion of continuing, professional education.

Knowles (1978) stated that learning in adults was quite different from that in children. He has since modified his view (1980) and now describes learning in terms of a continuum which develops as the individual matures. Inherent in Knowles' belief is that the term 'adult' relates to experience and maturity rather than just chronological age. However, his original thoughts regarding adults are still applicable in terms of the continuum of learning. According to Knowles (1978) adult education, or andragogy, is based upon four main assumptions.

1. That as a person grows and matures his self-concept moves from one of total dependency to one of increasing self-directedness. The point at which the individual achieves a concept of self-direction is the point at which he psychologically becomes an adult. At this point he then has a need to be perceived by others as self-directing and, if this does not happen, conflict then occurs.

2. That as the individual matures he accumulates an expanding reservoir of experience that causes him to become an increasingly rich resource for learning and, at the same time, provides him with a broadening base to which new learning can be related.

3. That as an individual matures, his readiness to learn is decreasingly the product of biological development and is increasingly the product of developing social roles, i.e. the job.

4. That adults have a problem-centred orientation to learning and have immediacy of application for what they are learning.

On review of these statements, it can be recognised that further debate and analysis are still required as, like any theory, they may be modified further in the light of new understanding. However, despite this, the intrinsic ideas contained in the statements are significant to individual nurse practitioners in relation to the facilitation of learning, teaching, curriculum design and, for that matter, all facets of education.

THE LEARNING PROCESSES AND RESOURCES

In the light of professional responsibilities, the concept of education, and availability of resources, it is necessary to identify and discuss ways by which nurses, in all roles, may continue to learn.

It is recognised that people learn by means of self-direction, facilitation, being taught, or through discussion. People also learn by being influenced, conditioned, or indoctrinated; however, these last three processes are not considered to be legitimate in terms of the current concept of education. All nurses, then, have a responsibility to themselves and to others to ensure that only learning processes which meet the criteria of education as previously defined are used.

Self-Directed Learning

Inherent in this process of learning is the individual's ability to self-motivate, to independently plan and execute learning programmes, and take full responsibility for outcomes. It implies a commitment to learning, such a commitment being recognised as a prerequisite of the members of any developing professional group. Self-directed learning meets the criteria of education outlined previously and is well suited to the adult learner as defined by Knowles (1978).

For the most part, in the past, learning has been associated with attendance at structured courses or study days. The content of these events has generally been defined by training bodies, managers or teachers, with little reference to the individual participants. Equally, participants and their managers have not always given enough consideration to the selection of appropriate courses from those available.

Self-directed learning does not preclude attendance on a course or a study day. However, it does ensure that the right course or study day is attended by the right person who has made a deliberate choice in relation to personal and professional learning needs.

For the most part, self-directed learning occurs through self-initiated actions such as reading, joining associations, attending conferences, and discussion. The self-directed learner also recognises and makes the most of all the available resources, such as distance learning material, the library and the experience of others.

In order to be recognised as professional practitioners, nurses must:

- Become increasingly more self-directing and take responsibility for their own learning
- Be able to recognise, make available, and use their own experience and the experience of others
- Be able to recognise their own learning needs and the learning needs of others in the light of their defined role
- Be able to plan and evaluate individual, self-directed learning programmes based upon the identified learning needs
- Ensure that statements relating to education and learning are included when conceptualising nursing (Olson and Kartha, 1983)

Activities of the self-directed learning process can be related to those of the action research model, as are the activities of the nursing process and the change process. Thus, a series of deliberate steps or stages can be identified, including:

- Self-assessment and identification of learning needs
- Setting of learning objectives
- Identification and selection of an appropriate learning strategy
- Implementation of the strategy
- Self-evaluation of outcomes in terms of the perceived objectives of learning

Learning by Facilitation

Professionals not only have a responsibility for their own learning but also for helping others learn. Knowles (1978) recognised the uniqueness of each of us in terms of our experience which, in itself, is the most valuable resource and which should be available to others.

'Help' and 'assist' are the key words in facilitation. The facilitator, then, may help and assist by acting as a resource, and in the creation of a climate or environment in which learning is acceptable, respectable and valued. Many nurses find that one of the most difficult things to do is actually to translate new ideas into practice or see ways through difficult problems which they have been able to identify, but not always solve. The role of a facilitator can be invaluable in this sort of situation, bringing fresh eyes to the problem, assisting in finding a solution without being judgmental in the suggestion of a right or wrong answer, and in providing the external interest and concern which are often required to help people to maintain the energy in seeing a new idea through.

Learning by Teaching

Teaching can only be considered legitimate, in terms of the concept of education, if the learner is central to the teaching process. Therefore, teaching is only concerned with that which the learner perceives as being relevant and/or appropriate. It is the learner who must be considered at all times. Obviously, this has implications for all nurses, since teaching is an integral part of nursing. Furthermore, it is the responsibility of all professional practitioners to help others within their profession to learn.

This could be an area of great conflict and difficulty since all of us have our own ideas about what people should know and be able to do, and these ideas are tied up with values, beliefs and personal learning experiences. Therefore, it is often the case that, when teaching, we may impose what we consider should be learned, thereby creating a teacher-centred as opposed to a learner-centred process.

Equally, a compromise on what should be taught will also need to be sought from among the opinions of all the learners, who will undoubtedly have different ideas. However, it must also be borne in mind that there are some aspects of learning which are essential to students before they can enter a profession and a responsibility does rest with teachers to ensure that they have a clear understanding of what these areas are. If this responsibility is not fulfilled, we would be failing in our duty to the public to ensure that all those who call themselves qualified nurses have reached an agreed level of learning.

Learning by Discussion

This process of learning again relies heavily on beliefs in the value of individuals and their experiences. Discussion is a two-way process where there is a planned interchange between two or more people, each individual both giving and taking in terms of the educational process.

Learning Contracts

Learning contracts relate to the recognition of desired learning outcomes. In terms of self-directed learning, the individual makes a contract with her or himself. However, in certain instances where the learner may have to account for learning, the contract may then be with a manager or teacher. As in all contractual situations, however, there are always responsibilities on both sides. On the part of the learner it may be the fulfilment of an agreed learning activity, and on the part of the teacher or manager there may be a responsibility to provide such things as time, resources or support and guidance.

Learning contracts identify learning objectives, learning strategies and evaluation strategies (Donald, 1976). The learning contract can be of great value when used in conjunction with performance review, where learning for an identified time period may be required (Keyser, 1986).

Resources

From the discussion of learning processes, the need for resources, in terms of time, money, people with appropriate experience, and support services such as libraries and teachers, becomes very evident.

Up to now, the so-called development of professionalism has not been matched with the necessary educational resources. Time granted for learning is kept to a minimum. It is nonsense to suggest that one day a year is sufficient time in which nurses can conceivably keep up to date: this was the time period suggested in the UKCC discussion document regarding mandatory refreshment (1987). It is recognised, however, that this was suggested as a day in addition to present levels of in-service updating. In the light of mandatory refreshment, it is necessary now to negotiate reasonable time periods, and it could be suggested that five days per year would be a more realistic minimum figure.

While there is undoubtedly some responsibility on the part of employers to ensure that a time allowance is made for continuing education, nurses also have a responsibility to give a little of their own time to their personal development. For example, surely it is not too much to expect that each person will read a professional journal each week, or from time to time attend a week-end conference without automatically expecting time back. Few professional practitioners work strictly 'to the clock' and there has to be some give-and-take in this situation.

Money is always limited, but it is an essential commodity with regard to the provision of many resources. However, by using resources efficiently, the maximum use of the money which is available can be more readily assured. In these days of economy and accountability, none of us can afford to be wasteful. Educational costs must be included in departmental budgeting. Realistic costing is essential if monies are to be assured for educational use. The old saying that we cannot afford it must now be superseded by stating clearly that we cannot afford to be without it.

Libraries are one of the most important resources for nurses as a source of information upon which clinical decisions can be based. Many practising nurses at the moment do not even have such a facility available to them and for others the service is inadequate, to say the least. It would appear that this kind of service is still seen as being non-essential and the comment often heard is that nurses do not use a library anyway. The defined role and responsibilities of the nurse of today, however, make it essential that up-to-date information is readily available upon which decisions are made and for which they may be held accountable.

EXERCISES

1. Identify those factors which help to create a learning environment and make a comparison with the reality of the clinical unit in which you work. Are there any steps you could take to bring the two closer together?

2. Using the concept of self-directed learning, identify a subject you would like to learn more about, then plan and work through a personal learning experience.

3. Discuss with the people you work with the possibility of introducing learning contracts during future performance reviews.

4. Identify ways in which you could act as a facilitator, making use of your own expertise and knowledge.

Further Reading

Iwasin C L (1987) The role of the teacher in self-directed learning. *Nurse Education Today*, **7**: 222–227.

Jarvis P (1983) *Professional Education*. London: Croom Helm.

Jarvis P (1985) *The Sociology of Adult and Continuing Education*. London: Croom Helm.

Puetz B (1985) *Evaluation in Nursing Staff Development: Method and Models*. Rockville, MD: Aspen Systems Corporation.

9
Using Research in Nursing

The purpose of this chapter is to help you to:

- Be able to define research and identify the steps in the research process
- Be familiar with some of the terms commonly used in research
- Have some ideas about how research can be introduced into practice

For some time now there has been a growing interest in the use of research in nursing. The Briggs Report (1972) recommended that nursing should be a research-based occupation, and there has been a steady increase in the number of people who are paying serious attention to the important contribution that research can play in clinical care. So what is this thing called research, and how can we make use of it in our everyday lives?

In very simple terms, research can be described as an activity which attempts to find answers to questions; in other words, it is a systematic way of approaching a problem when we are not sure of the solution and are seeking an answer. However, this definition does leave itself open to some misunderstanding.

It is not uncommon to hear people say that they must 'do some research' to investigate such things as mouth care, information-giving or the management of pressure areas. In fact, there is a considerable amount of research-based information already available in relation to these areas of nursing. This is not to suggest that the 'ultimate answer' to mouth care, or any of the other topics, has been found, but that many people have already undertaken work in this area. So the first step in answering a problem of this nature is to 'search' systematically through the literature to see if any one has already come up with a solution.

An approach of this kind is not research itself, but the recognition and use of other people's work. It is certainly a practice that many of us take advantage of in other walks of life. For example, if one wanted to buy a new washing machine or video recorder it is unlikely that one would spend hours investigating all the different options available at first hand, but it would be both sensible and time-saving to consult a recent copy of *Which?*, where someone has already undertaken the hard work on our behalf and published the findings for our benefit. In the same way, when we come across a clinical problem it is both logical and time-saving to see what other people have to say before making our own judgment about how to act.

This level of research is known as research appreciation or awareness, that is the ability to interpret, criticise and, when appropriate, make use of other people's work. It is a fundamental skill which is required of any professional practitioner and is particularly important in current nursing with a growing awareness of accountability for practice and the need to make defensible decisions about nursing actions. Gone are the days when it was sufficient to say, 'We've always done it that way'. We are now in the age where our actions are questioned and we must be able to put forward a reasonable rationale for the way in which we practise.

If demands of this kind are being made upon us, it becomes important that all nurses should not only be aware of research that has been undertaken but should also be able to interpret that research, make a judgment about its usefulness and decide whether or not it would be of value in a particular clinical setting. Just like any other topic, not all research is good, nor is all work 'transferable' from one setting to another. Inappropriate use of research can be, at the simplest level, wasteful, and at the worst level, dangerous.

For many nurses practising today, an understanding of research was not included in basic nurse education, so it is a skill which has had to be developed at a later stage. Yet it is not as complex as many people think at first sight. Research, like many other things, is a process with a series of identifiable stages. A fuller and more apt description than the one given earlier is:

> 'An attempt to find answers to questions through a sequence of steps, including mental activity, designed to increase the sum of what is known . . . by the discovery of new facts or the relationship between things.' (Cormack, 1984)

The fundamental difference about research is that it goes beyond 'what I know', which can be expanded by study or investigation. Research seeks to expand the sum of 'what is known' – in other words, an attempt is made to increase the total sum of knowledge.

Figure 9.1 (p. 124) identifies the steps in the research process, at each stage giving an indication of the points which should be taken into consideration either when reading other people's work or undertaking a personal study. It is only a general guide, since there are always variations which are relevant in different circumstances, but it is a useful beginning.

THE LANGUAGE OF RESEARCH

Like many other people, including nurses, researchers have a 'language' of their own, using words which may be familiar to us in other contexts but which have a specific meaning when used in relation to research. Some of the commonly used words are given below with a brief description of their meanings.

Design

This refers to the overall plan or pattern of the research and the way in which it was carried out. There are some broad design patterns which most, but not all, studies fit into. Recognition of the patterns gives some indication of how the information can be used. Common design approaches include the following.

1. *Historical research*   A systematic review of data available from the past but interpreted in a new light with different associations being made. Information gathered from historical studies can be invaluable when planning for the future. Factors which have influenced past events can be taken into account, as well as the effectiveness of the strategies applied.

2. *Descriptive research (surveys)*   In this case, information is sought about current practice, the reality of what is happening here and now. It is easy to make assumptions about practice without having any real evidence, and the findings of some surveys can be very surprising. They give information which can be very useful as a basis for planning developments, learning programmes or, indeed, further research.

3. *Experimental research*   In experimental research an attempt is made to control a variable (see page 124) by either introducing it or removing it under controlled conditions in order to see whether or not it has an effect on a particular situation. For example, you may choose to investigate the use of a new mouth-wash lotion by using it with one group of patients while making no changes for another, and assessing the effects of the two procedures.

4. *Action research*   This is a method whereby the researcher feeds information to a group throughout the research process which is aimed at solving a problem in a systematic way. Unlike other

	Doing research	Reading research
The question or problem	Where did the problem originate and is it worth following? How are the terms defined, e.g. does 'nurse' include qualified and unqualified staff?	Is the problem and the purpose of the study clearly stated? Are the terms defined?
Limitations	What time, skills and money are available?	Who funded the study? May this lead to bias? Who undertook the study? Was this appropriate?
Literature search	Does the literature already provide an answer to the problem? What background knowledge is required?	Does the report show wide reading around the subject? Are both positive and negative arguments presented?
Assumptions	Are any assumptions being made? Can they be justified?	Are any assumptions made? Are they justified?
Aims (hypothesis)	What are the aims of the study? What variables are made? How do they relate to original problem/question? Is a hypothesis needed?	Do the aims of the study relate to the original problem? Are the variables identified? Is the hypothesis stated (only necessary in experimental research)?
Sample	What sample will be studied? Is it representative of total population? What numbers are needed to give reliable information?	How was the sample population identified? Was it representative of the total population? What was the number involved and the response rate achieved?
Design	What is the most appropriate design of study (historical, descriptive, experimental, action, etc.)?	What design of study was used? Was this an appropriate choice to answer the question?
Method	What is the most appropriate method,	What method was used and why was it

	Doing research	Reading research
	bearing in mind the limitations? How will data be analysed?	chosen? Are the 'tools' available?
Ethical points	Is the study ethically acceptable; should the local ethics committee be consulted? How will options for involvement be given?	Are ethical considerations discussed? How were participants given a choice of involvement?
Pilot study	How can the method be tested? How will data be analysed?	Was the pilot study completed? Did it lead to modification of the method used?
Data collection	Who will collect data? How will bias be excluded? Has the researcher the time available?	Who collected data? Was bias considered?
Analysis	How will data be analysed? What are the cost/skills implications? What statistical tests are needed, if any?	Is the method of analysis understandable? Is explanation of statistical tests given?
Results	These must be kept separate from conclusions and presented as exact report of findings. Graphs, tables, etc. help.	Are 'raw' figures and percentages included? Is exact data presented?
Conclusions	What conclusions can be drawn? How can they be justified? How do they relate to the aims of the study?	Does the conclusion relate to the original questions? Are the aims achieved? Are the conclusions based on the actual findings?
Recommendations	What recommendations can be made for change and development?	Are recommendations justifiable? Are they 'transferable' to the reader's area? Should she be acting on them?

Fig 9.1   The research process. Adapted from Hawthorne P (1983) 'Principles of Research – checklist', *Nursing Times*, **79**(35), pp. 41–43.

types of research, the desired outcome is not expressed in strict terms at the beginning, and the plan of the project is developed in the light of evidence from each stage.

5. *Ethnographic research*   Ethnography refers to the study of a particular group or culture, either by one of its own members or an outsider, in order to be able to describe the characteristics of the group. Information is usually gathered either by observation of the group or by interpretation of their conversation. Valuable insight can be gained in this way to help understand how the group under study function, which can be used in planning for the future.

Variables

A variable is a characteristic which can be modified or altered. 'Extraneous variables' are all those things which may influence the findings in a study, such as variations in the backgrounds of the staff, differences in the patient population or the facilities available in the clinical setting. Account should be made of them in any study design.

In experimental studies, reference may be made to an 'independent variable', the thing which is introduced or manipulated by the researcher; and a 'dependent variable', the thing which may be affected by the independent variable. An example would be the effect of information-giving (independent variable) on the amount of pain (dependent variable).

Method

The research method refers to the way in which information was gathered and analysed during the study. The most commonly used methods are observation, interview and questionnaire.

1. *Observation*   Observation is actually watching what is happening and recording the events in order to be able to analyse them. It can be made up of one specific activity, such as the number of times hand-washing occurs, or of a broader number of events. Observers may either participate in activities or watch in as unobtrusive a way as possible from a distance.

2. *Interview*   An interviewer may approach an interviewee and seek information either following a formal, preplanned schedule or by talking in a freer manner about the topic under investigation. Sometimes interviews are recorded and at other times notes are taken. It can be a very time-consuming method of gathering information but can also lead to a depth of information which may be lost if other methods are used.

3. *Questionnaire* This is probably the commonest method used, since a large number of people can be reached in a relatively short space of time. However, it is not so easy to gain the same depth of information as at interview. Furthermore, good questionnaires are not easy to prepare and false assumptions can be made if the wrong questions are asked or they are badly worded. The design of questionnaires can vary enormously but it is vital that whichever form is used it is tested, or 'piloted', first with a group of people similar to the group to be used in the main study.

Sample

The 'sample' refers to the section of the population which was studied. The important things to note about the sample are the number of people involved and the manner in which they were chosen. Samples should be representative of the total population under study and can influence the 'transferability' of the findings. For example, findings relating to the eating habits of teenagers cannot be applied to an elderly population. However, if the design and method of a study are sound, a small sample can give rise to important findings.

Validity

Validity means the certainty with which a tool measures what it says it does. For example, asking a nurse, 'Are you kind to patients?' will not necessarily tell you whether the subject *actually* is kind to patients, it will only tell you whether the person sees him or herself as kind.

Reliability

Reliability refers to the consistency with which the findings occur using the same tool. Since there is a variation in the size of the bore of mercury thermometers and, hence, they reach the peak temperature recording at different rates, reliability can only be guaranteed if the same thermometer is used consistently throughout a study or several are tested before the study begins to see if they match. If this precaution is not taken it may legitimately be queried whether temperatures taken at different times using different thermometers can usefully be compared.

Obviously, there are many other terms which are commonly seen in research reports and it is impossible to give them all here. However, many books are now available which include a glossary of terms – some of these are listed at the end of this chapter.

USING RESEARCH IN PRACTICE

Once an insight into research appreciation has been gained, the question must be raised about how it can be introduced to everyday clinical practice. This is not to suggest that all clinical nurses should actually 'do' research, but that research findings which are relevant to their particular sphere of practice should be readily available for reference and incorporated into care planning. Ways in which this can be achieved are not complex and, while they may take a bit of extra time and commitment to initiate, once established they can be maintained relatively easily.

Literature Reviews

Many journals and some books contain literature searches on specific clinical topics; for example, work has been published in relation to recovery from illness (Wilson-Barnett and Fordham, 1982) and to pressure sores (Torrance, 1983).

On the whole, people who write such articles have given a considerable amount of time to the production of the work and are only too pleased that others should benefit by their efforts. After all, there is little point in re-inventing the wheel, and it is important that we recognise the work of others.

Journal Clubs

Filing articles about subjects which are relevant to the ward is one way to begin to keep up to date with new information. However, this does mean that the nursing journals have to be read regularly and appropriate articles identified. In some instances, a team of people can form a journal club sharing both the cost of the journals and the responsibility for scanning for appropriate articles. The importance of having a named person responsible for a named task has been stressed earlier in this book; this is one situation where each qualified member of the team may choose to take responsibility for a particular journal, bringing appropriate articles to the attention of colleagues to discuss whether they should be included in the file.

Literature Searching

While the use of other people's work is a good starting point, one may well become dissatisfied with this approach after a while and wish to be more systematic in the field of literature searching. Alternatively, it may not be possible to find a recent review on a particular subject that is relevant to the practice area. In this case, the answer may well be for one member of the team to investigate the literature personally.

There is often a feeling that it is the sister/charge nurse's responsibility to provide information on all aspects of practice but, in reality, it is neither reasonable nor possible for one person to be the expert in all areas of care. By offering the responsibility for gathering information about specific areas of nursing to each of the qualified members of the team, one may well end up with 'experts' in several different subjects who are in a position to share their new-found knowledge with one another.

Storing Information

Card indexes recording references for the literature and a summary of the topic can be kept for free access by both current and future team members and, in many instances, it may be found that members of other disciplines become interested in the rationale on which nursing practice is based. Articles identified through the journal club may be stored in this way.

The topics which have been mentioned so far have been mainly concerned with physical aspects of care but there is no reason why they should be confined in this way: indeed, it is highly desirable that information related to psychosocial aspects of nursing, such as coping with bereavement, are also included.

Some people may not be familiar with the way in which a literature search is undertaken since this was not a widely practised skill among nurses in times gone by; however, there are several sources of help which are readily available to most clinical nurses.

First, a colleague from the school of nursing who is familiar with the use of libraries and literature searching can be approached and asked for help. Alternatively, the local librarian may be able to indicate the right path to take. While librarians may not know much about the particular topic of interest and will need advice on such things as words which have similar meanings (e.g. pressure sore or bed sore) they are experts in handling the literature and seeking information. Third, there are publications which can be of help in gaining literature-searching skills, such as 'How to Find Information', available through the Royal College of Nursing.

If none of these routes is open, or developing research skills is a subject of particular interest, one can choose to go a step further. Many local education institutes offer short courses in study skills which often include advice on library use. Alternatively, distance learning material is now available (e.g. from the Distance Learning Centre) which can be studied at one's own pace and convenience.

While some of the suggestions given may seem to entail much effort, the end results are well worth while and research, rather than being an ivory-tower activity for other people, can become an everyday way of thinking within clinical practice. All this implies is that there is a curiosity and questioning about how and why we do certain things and a desire to discover the reasoning behind nursing actions rather than an acceptance of them through habit and tradition.

Inevitably, when practice is challenged in this way, there will be times when the answers that are sought are not readily available, and in this situation it might be that the time has come to go beyond the stage of research appreciation to research action. Many of the important subjects which have been raised in nursing research are those which have arisen out of the questions and hunches of clinical nurses, even though the researchers themselves have been employed in non-clinical jobs. So, if such a hunch comes along, what can be done about it?

First of all, it may well be worth while to write a letter to one of the nursing journals expressing your interest. It could be that someone else has had similar thoughts or feelings and has already begun to investigate the topic. Alternatively, the idea may be picked up by someone in a more formal research post, starting a chain of thought which could lead to an investigation at a later date.

Once you have become familiar with the research process, there is no reason why small-scale studies cannot be initiated in your unit. However, it is strongly recommended that if you should choose to do this but are inexperienced, you should seek advice and help before beginning in order to be sure of going about things in such a way as to gather usable information. But do not be put off by this: the findings from studies of this nature may not be transferable but may well be sufficient to provide the answers to a local clinical problem. For example, a simple survey about visitors' experiences in travelling to the hospital may give ideas about the policy for visiting, or a record of the amount of warning given to allow time for discharge planning may be helpful when negotiating with medical colleagues on this aspect of clinical management.

The examples which could be given are never-ending, but all that is being done is making use of a knowledge of the research process in everyday practice.

Some of the main issues in research have been described in this chapter, and a few ideas offered about raising research awareness in practice. These are only intended as an introduction, and recommendations for further reading are given below.

However, as a final word, it is worth saying that the major resistance to research stems from uncertainty and fear and, once these obstacles are overcome, research can become an invaluable asset to the improvement of the quality of care and an essential background to clinical practice.

EXERCISES

1. Using the guidelines given in Figure 9.1, read and analyse a research article from one of the nursing journals. Persuade one of your colleagues to read the same article and compare your ideas.

2. Make a list of at least six clinical topics which are relevant to your practice. Discuss each one with the people with whom you work, in each case to explore the rationale on which practice is based. See if there are any variations in ideas and try to discover the source of the knowledge on which the recommendations are based.

3. Undertake a literature search related to one of the topics identified earlier where the rationale for practice was unclear. Start a file and/or card index of the articles you found to be helpful.

4. Over the next six months, build up a file and card index of information relating to each of the clinical topics identified in Exercise 2. See whether each of the qualified members of the team of nurses will take responsibility for one subject in order to share the workload, and give everyone a chance to contribute.

Further Reading

Cormack D (ed.) (1984) *The Research Process in Nursing.* Oxford: Blackwell Scientific Publications.

Macleod Clark J and Hockey L (1979) *Research for Nursing – A Guide for the Enquiring Nurse.* Chichester: HM+M/John Wiley and Sons.

Nieswiadorny R (1986) *Foundations of Nursing Research.* New York: Appleton–Century.

Polit D F and Hunglar B P (1985) *Essentials of Nursing Research – Methods and Application.* Philadelphia: J B Lippincott.

Treece E W and Treece J W (1975) *Elements of Research in Nursing.* St Louis: C V Mosby.

10
Taking the Strain

This chapter aims to introduce you to:

- Ways of recognising common responses to stress
- The manifestations of stress at ward level
- Ways of minimising the effects of stress

WHAT IS STRESS?

Imagine this scene – you are walking down the main shopping street in town and notice a friend in the shop opposite. When you are half way across the road a car horn sounds and you see a car coming quickly towards you. What happens next? What does it feel like? Just think about this for a moment. It is likely that:

- You are feeling wide awake, alert, and aware of all your surroundings, especially the car
- You are frightened and anxious
- Your heart is pounding
- Your breathing is fast
- Your mouth is dry
- Your skin has become cold and clammy
- Your muscles are tense . . .

and you run out of the way of the car.

What has been described is the classic response to stress. It is an instinctive reaction to a life-threatening situation and is vital for survival. This basically physiological response prepares the individual either to fight or to run away, hence its alternative name, the 'fight or flight' response.

The Fight or Flight Response

Following the initial perception of danger, interconnected physiological mechanisms are activated which result in an increase in secretion of epinephrine and an increase in adrenergic activity of the autonomic nervous system. The net effect of these physiological responses is to promote a maximum state of alertness and to prepare the body for action.

The usefulness of this response is obvious where the threat to the individual is such that running away or fighting is the appropriate course of action. Unfortunately, however, this automatic physiological response is evoked in other situations where fight or flight is inappropriate, such as in a traffic jam, a crowded lift or a dentist's waiting room. In these cases the biological imperative to fight or run is overborne by higher cortical activity in recognition of other demands such as good manners or an aching tooth! Other quite trivial events like noisy children or the bus being late again can spark off the automatic reaction and, for some people, this type of response can become exaggerated into a generalised habit.

The events or situations which trigger stress reactions are very variable and wide-ranging and are known as stressors. For example, public speaking, returning damaged articles to a shop, starting a new job or asking for a pay rise are all activities which may be experienced as stressful. A number of themes are evident, however, such as:

- *Threat of physical danger* to oneself or others, as in road accidents, before major surgery or in mountaineering
- *Loss* of any description such as divorce, redundancy, amputation or imprisonment
- *Loss* of face or self-esteem
- *Conflict* between individuals, between roles or between groups
- *Change* of any kind, as in adolescence, early motherhood, or a new work role
- *Obstacles* to the achievement of life goals

It is important to note that it is the way these events are perceived which leads to stress and that even the possibility that one of them might occur can precipitate the experience. Studies of life events have shown that even events which might be considered happy and positive, such as marriage, winning the football pools or even taking a holiday, can be stressful (Holmes and Rahe, 1967). It has been suggested that it is the degree of mental or physical adjustment required which is one of the determinants of the level of stress experienced.

IS STRESS BAD FOR YOU?

The answer to this question is 'yes and no'! Stress can be very positive and productive, leading to:

- Increased effort
- Improved performance
- Problem-solving activities
- Feelings of stimulation and excitement – the 'highs'
- Satisfaction when the situation is resolved – the 'glow'

While acute stress may be uncomfortable for a short time, repeated, prolonged or severe stress may lead to more harmful consequences. These negative effects of stress show themselves in a number of ways, physically, emotionally and socially: the range of responses is vast and varies from person to person. The responses result not only from the direct effects of the stress itself but also from attempts by the individual to cope with the unpleasant sensations and feelings that are generated. These efforts at coping, such as heavy drinking, may often create other problems in their turn. Common negative effects of stress include:

- Sleep and appetite disturbance, tiredness, lethargy, nausea, vomiting, headaches, frequent colds, loss of libido, indigestion, constipation and 'butterflies'
- Anxiety, depression, panic, apathy, anger, irritability, boredom, helplessness, feeling out of control, tension, loss of concentration, poor memory, confusion, over reactivity
- Absenteeism, poor time-keeping, accidents, heavy drinking, taking drugs, gambling, criminal activity, social withdrawal

Often other changes in behaviour may be observed in someone under stress, and it is usually the fact that change has occurred which is as significant as the behaviour being shown. For example, a talkative person may become quiet and secretive or a good time-keeper suddenly starts to be late for meetings.

Although it is still a controversial subject, it has been suggested that stress may play a part in triggering or maintaining a number of physical and mental illnesses. Figure 10.1 gives an indication of the wide spread of conditions thought to be associated in some way with stress.

Who is Prone to Stress?

Different people appear to respond to stress in different ways. Individuals may differ in their physiological response owing to hereditary factors, early learning experiences or specific organ vulnerability. It has also been suggested that some personalities suffer more from the effects of stress than others. So-called 'Type A' personalities, that is those who are competitive, aggressive and industrious, have been associated with higher levels of coronary

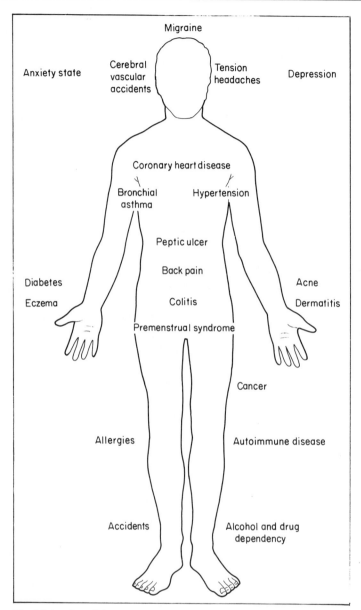

Fig 10.1 Conditions associated with stress

heart disease than 'Type B' personalities who are calm, relaxed and phlegmatic. A reduction in Type A behaviour in favour of Type B is said to decrease the likelihood of the worst effects of stress.

Variability in Stress

Factors relating to the stress itself may also influence the degree to which ill effects are experienced by the individual. Such factors include:

- The meaning of the event
- The degree of control over the situation
- The predictability of the event
- The availability of support

This variability in both the response to stress and the experience of the ill effects suggests that it is possible to modify stress responses, and research on biofeedback and relaxation training has shown this to be the case. In laboratory experiments volunteers were able to reduce both their blood pressure and their heart rate by the use of techniques taught by the experimenters (Schwartz, 1975).

STRESS AND GROUPS

Groups also respond to stress in characteristic ways. For example, an external threat may lead to greater cohesiveness in a group by reaffirming a common goal, by allowing the expression of shared feelings or by giving the group an agreed target for hostility, as in wartime. Thus, in a work situation a temporary shortage of staff may lead to increased effort, closer teamwork and higher morale. However, when stress is prolonged or when there is little initial cohesion, fragmentation and disorganisation ensue, resulting in ineffective teamwork, abrasive relationships, poor performance and low morale.

It has also been shown, notably by Isabel Menzies in 1960, that organisations develop their own formal ways of reducing stress and anxiety. Menzies, in her study of the nursing service of a large teaching hospital, described the development of patterns of nursing care and management which had the apparent effect of reducing the overall levels of anxiety felt by the nursing staff. One strategy she described involved the 'splitting of the nurse–patient relationship' by the use of task allocation. Others involved 'ritualised task performance, depersonalisation and denial of the significance of the individual', whether nurse or patient.

Although it has been suggested that these types of institutional responses to stress have been fairly effective, especially in terms of the organisation as a whole, they have frequently created problems for the individuals concerned. In recent years, trends in nursing, such as the move to primary nursing, have led to the abandonment of many of these strategies. Although some have suggested that the very closeness of the nurse–patient relationship can be an effective support in itself (Benner, 1984), alternate and effective methods have not been widely adopted.

In summary, each individual responds in his or her own way to stress which in itself is unavoidable and a part of everyday life. However, the effects of stress can be both beneficial and harmful, action being required if:

- Everyday functioning is affected
- Relationships begin to deteriorate
- Productivity or performance begin to decline
- Decision-making becomes impaired

STRESS IN NURSING

'Nursing has long been recognised as a profession in which personalised and institutional stresses are inherent': so stated a working party of the Royal College of Nursing in 1978. While few would disagree, little appears to have been done to remedy the matter.

Sources of stress are not hard to find. Some relate to the very nature of the work, such as close and repeated contact with the dying and with bereaved relatives. Others relate to work conditions and the responses of others to the job: for example, low pay, unsocial hours, shift-work and low status can all be factors which can be stressful.

A particularly striking source of stress is that of the unrealistically high expectations generated by nurses both of themselves and of others. This discrepancy between the ideal and what it is possible to achieve produces a good deal of dissatisfaction and frustration. Cox (1978) describes work stress as 'a dynamic and individual phenomenon rooted in the person's appraisal of the degree to which he is matched to his environment'. Nurses, while understandably attempting to give the high standard of care expected by their colleagues, the public and, most importantly, themselves, can in reality seldom succeed.

Changes in medical care and developments in nursing have also led to increased pressure. Tschudin (1985) has identified four recent trends:

- The introduction of the nursing process, re-establishing the relationship between individual nurses and individual patients

- The increasing use of 'high-tech' equipment, leading not only to the need for increased technical skill and knowledge but also for a greater awareness of the ethical issues involved
- Patients are becoming increasingly knowledgeable and desirous of participation in their own nursing care, which has meant a change of role for many nurses
- Recurrent reorganisations and increased pressure on resources

Hingley and Harris (1986), when looking at the problems faced by nurse managers, have suggested another series of stressors. Some of these are related to relationships and communication at work such as poor feedback from senior colleagues, lack of social supports and lack of involvement in decision-making. Others relate to their role in the organisation, such as role conflict and role ambiguity. The conflicts between the demands of home and work were also frequently mentioned, especially by women with dependent children.

The list is endless but, despite what may appear to be an overwhelming situation, nurses do cope. It is clear, however, that they do not cope without some cost to themselves or their families and the profession. High levels of wastage and dropout have long been a cause for concern. Life expectancy for nurses is about two years less than that for other comparable professions and nurses, alongside other health workers, rank high in occupational mortality statistics for causes of death such as suicide and the adverse effects of drugs (OPCS, 1978).

The concept of 'burnout' as an end result of stress is highly relevant in this context. Burnout refers to a state of physical and emotional exhaustion characterised according to Maslach (1982) by a change in attitude, '. . . a shift from the positive and caring to the negative and uncaring'. Early stages of this condition are said to be recognisable by irritability, perceiving patients as demanding, working after hours and feeling indispensable. It is inevitable that both nurses and patients must suffer if this is allowed to happen.

Manifestations of Stress on the Ward

It should now be clear that the effects of stress on individual nurses, other members of the staff and the ward as a whole can be recognised quite easily. A nurse under stress may become miserable or anxious, uncharacteristically late, accident-prone or may begin to take uncertificated sick leave. She may simply seem less caring. If this situation is allowed to go unrecognised it may well spread to other staff, for there is no doubt that it is contagious, and low morale and a breakdown in working relationships may occur. A general increase in absenteeism, poor time-keeping and complaints may be noted, as well as a decrease in effective, productive work in the face of apparent effort.

When this occurs, the time has come to act (although prevention is better than cure!). If no action is taken, the result may be a high and rapid turnover of staff, poor recruitment and an increase in stress for those remaining. Patient care, of course, will inevitably suffer.

Minimising Stress

The need to reduce stress in nursing is clear. It can be done. It is possible to learn new ways of coping and even to change the habits of a lifetime. In the following section a number of different strategies are suggested to help the nurse to reduce stress. They are divided to correspond roughly with the demands of the roles which most workers occupy, namely that of worker, carer and manager, and that most important aspect, the nurse as an individual, is not forgotten.

It is useful to distinguish at this stage between two types of coping or 'taking the strain'. *Defensive strategies* are those which attempt to minimise the unpleasant side effects of stress such as anxiety and muscular tension: they include such things as drinking heavily or taking tranquillisers. *Coping strategies*, on the other hand, are those methods by which the individual attempts to avoid or resolve the stressful situation, for instance by using problem-solving techniques. Everyone uses a combination of defensive and coping strategies and each has its advantages. Coping strategies may lead to the successful removal of a source of stress but, when stress cannot be avoided or resolved, defensive strategies clearly have a protective function.

Most of the foregoing discussion assumes that the responsibility for coping with stress lies with the individual. Although it is both feasible and in the nurse's best interest to cope effectively, it is also in the interest of the organisation for stress to be kept within manageable limits, and in this respect management has a role. This may not always be accepted or recognised, and there may be times when nurses need to put pressure on other members of the team or organisation so that action is taken. This may not be easy, but a well-reasoned argument backed by evidence may produce widespreading and positive results for both staff and patients.

The suggestions below may not apply to everyone and those tips not felt to be immediately relevant may be left for a future occasion. Individuals may perhaps like to make a note of their own particular ideas and wrinkles to add to this list.

THE NURSE AS A PERSON

To cope with the demands of a job and life in general it makes sense to ensure that your basic equipment, your mind and body, is in good working order. Being fit and being able to relax can help you to resist or throw off the worst effects of stress. Good social or other leisure interests can act as a counterbalance to the demands of everyday life.

A Healthy Body

1. *Eat well,* eat a varied diet and do not be tempted to skip meals.

2. Watch your intake of *caffeine,* which lurks in cola drinks and chocolate as well as tea and coffee. It is a stimulant and may lead to palpitations and difficulty in sleeping.

3. *Alcohol* in small amounts does help you to relax but excess can lead to damage to the liver, the digestive and the nervous systems as well as leaving you with a hangover!
   The Health Education Authority suggests that a man should keep his weekly intake to under 20 units and a woman to under 13. One unit is said to be the equivalent of half a pint of beer, one single measure of spirits or one glass of wine.

4. Try to reduce your *smoking.* Although smoking is often seen as an aid to relaxation, the dangers to health in the long term greatly outweigh the benefits. But do not create more problems by trying to give it up when under stress.

5. Get enough *sleep.* Learn how much you need and arrange to get it. Being physically tired might help but do not worry about not sleeping – it will only make matters worse.

6. Get enough *exercise.* It will not only help you to feel fitter, more energetic and more able to cope with the physical work but it will also help you to relax, work off pent-up emotions and sleep well.

7. Do not ignore your *general health.* Have check-ups at the dentist, where necessary, and see your doctor if minor symptoms persist. No-one will look after your health if you do not.

Learn to Relax

1. *Muscular tension* can lead to headaches, high blood pressure, tiredness and inability to sleep.

2. Try taking a *long bath*, take the dog for a walk – or what about a massage?

3. If *mental relaxation* is also wanted try yoga, t'ai chi or transcendental meditation.

4. Take all your *holidays* and enjoy them. You do not have to go away but try to do something different.

5. If you want to learn something more about *relaxation* and how to care for yourself, try locally-run night classes entitled 'Look After Yourself', or similar programmes. You may also be able to find commercially-produced audio-tapes which teach relaxation.

A Positive Attitude

1. *Have confidence in yourself*, but set yourself realistic goals. Do not expect too much of yourself.

2. *Do not bottle up your feelings.* Keeping quiet can be quite counterproductive. Anger, particularly, must be expressed in some way – by being assertive or by taking direct action. You can also work it out of your system by exercise, such as scrubbing the floor or beating the carpet.

3. *Find someone in whom you can confide* and talk to him or her. If a friend or relative is not available try your local doctor or clergyman – but do talk to someone.

4. *Remember that most crises are survivable* and although you may come out a little dented, you will come out.

THE NURSE AS A WORKER

Nursing is a job, no matter how dedicated you are, and nurses are workers. This implies certain rights and responsibilities. Employers have the right to expect a good day's work but, equally, workers have the right not to be exploited.

1. *Define and clarify your role.* Do not exceed that role in any other than exceptional circumstances. This does not mean you cannot be flexible but flexibility needs to be defined, too.

2. *Monitor your own performance,* and get feedback if necessary. Try to identify gaps in your knowledge or experience and correct them.

3. *Develop good working relationships,* but do not expect everyone to be friendly. Get to know the system and use it.

4. *Take your holidays,* breaks, time off and so forth. You do no-one any good by overtiring yourself.

5. *Monitor the effects of shift work,* especially when changes from day to night are frequent.

6. *Try to separate home and work,* either in terms of time or distance. If you live on site, try shopping or playing badminton before going home.

7. *If you feel bored* or restless, reassess your position, checking with others if necessary. 'Rustout' can be just as harmful as burnout. A research project or short course may reawaken your interest.

8. *If you have a complaint,* go through the appropriate procedures and contact your professional body or union.

9. *Remember you are more than what you do:* you must have a life outside nursing.

THE NURSE AS A CARER

All nurses set themselves high standards and these are reinforced by the public who need to feel that nurses can cope, no matter what. This is clearly not the case, since nurses have strengths and weaknesses, good and bad days, just like everyone else. Nurses have emotions, too, and can get angry, upset and sad. If patients are to be treated as people, nurses must treat themselves like people also.

1. *You have limitations;* recognise them. It is not possible to be good at everything or to solve all problems. Just do what you can.

2. *Talk to others about the way you feel.* Find someone on the ward or unit you can talk to. This may be the sister, the ward clerk or the chaplain, but share your feelings. You will find that you are not alone.

3. *Do not be afraid of feeling.* Tears do not foretell doom and disaster. Put yourself first occasionally.

4. *Learn to cope with the unexpected.* Try to be aware of the least likely turns of events and prepare for them in advance. Be prepared to improvise.

5. *Consider seeking a formal network on the ward.* A staff group or co-counselling may be useful. Try contacting the school of nursing, the social work department or even the psychiatric unit for advice or help in setting these up.

THE NURSE AS A MANAGER

Often the loneliest role a nurse can have, the manager has to manage, to make decisions and to be responsible. It is the manager who experiences most conflict between roles and yet is often without direct day-to-day support.

For yourself:
- Develop a comfortable management style – do not try to be what you are not.
- Learn about and use the system.
- Learn to delegate without watching over people's shoulders.
- Develop relationships with other staff which both sides are happy with.
- Seek out support. It may come from the 'hierarchy', from other units or colleagues in similar roles.
- If you recognise problems, do seek help, training or support early. Be assertive and ask for what you want.

For others:
- Try to know your staff so that you can recognise when they are under stress.
- Be accessible: keep communication channels open and listen to what is being said.
- Give positive feedback whenever possible. A simple 'thank you' is much appreciated and vastly productive of good will.
- Introduce changes slowly after full consultation with other staff. Some practice or rehearsal may help.
- Consider setting up staff support groups on the ward.
- Be prepared to pressure the organisation for adequate staffing and resources, counselling and support services.
- Be prepared to spend time with your staff – it is what being a manager is about.

There are many other roles which a nurse may adopt – teacher, clinician, student, researcher. Unfortunately, the demands of each of these roles may conflict. There can be no formal rules to determine how the conflicts may be resolved but, in most clinical areas, the immediate needs of patients are usually the agreed priority. However, this may not always be appropriate and good judgment and a flexible approach may be necessary. Following an unsuccessful attempt at resuscitation, for example, time must be found for the nursing staff to talk and perhaps relieve pent-up emotions. If priorities are not immediately apparent, talk things over with colleagues, but sometimes it is worth trusting your instinct.

WHEN ALL ELSE FAILS . . .

When all else fails, it may be that the time has come to consider getting professional help. Most people reach a crisis point at some time in their lives. Counselling may be obtainable through the local doctor, occupational health department or through locally-organised counselling services. The Citizens' Advice Bureau may also be able to suggest local services. It is important to discuss the situation *before* taking drastic action such as handing in one's notice – this may, however, be the ultimate outcome if stress at work becomes both intolerable and resistant to all attempts to change it.

EXERCISES

Exercises 1–3 are designed to help you to become more aware, primarily of your own responses to stress, and to highlight both positive and negative coping mechanisms. The exercises can be adapted to focus on a group of nurses or other staff and you may wish to make alterations to suit your own circumstances.

Exercise 4 is designed to provide you with a resource file for use when major problems occur. Once completed, it may be appropriate to keep a copy on the ward.

Please take your time over these exercises. They are not intended as 'once and for all' activities. In the light of changing experience or skill in the future, you may wish to return to them and approach them in a new light. Good luck!

1. From your past experiences, identify and list your usual responses to stress, whether at home or at work. The following headings may be useful:

• Physical responses
• Emotional responses

Stress diary	Mary Baker, Staff Nurse			Date May 29th 1988
Time	Event	Response	Coping strategy	Alternative strategy (written later)
08.00	Numerous phone calls all through handover	Irritability/annoyance	Shouted at domestic supervisor over phone	Arrange for phone calls to be taken by ward clerk during handover
10.45	Complaints in middle of ward round from consultant in front of everyone about patient not being ready (in bath)	Embarrassed, felt guilty but annoyed	Blamed it on SEN and students	Discuss ward routine with consultant on one-to-one basis to consider nursing priorities. Also see if nursing staff could have planned their work differently
13.35	Phoned nursing officer for extra staff nurse to cover sickness on evening staff - refused	Anger	Acquiescence - no use fighting with nursing officer. Simmered, panicked all afternoon and got off duty late	Be more assertive with nursing officer. Discuss officially with nurse. Rearrange priorities of nursing work to see if non-essential activities can be left

Fig 10.2 Diary layout

- Cognitive responses
- Social responses

This exercise should not take more than about 20 minutes.

2. Complete a diary each day for three consecutive working days using Figure 10.2 or a copy as a guide but omitting column 5 'alternative strategies'. Each time you feel under stress indicate:

- The stressor – that is the stressful situation or events causing you to react (the event)
- Your initial emotional/cognitive response with any accompanying physical symptoms (the response)
- How you handled the situation (coping strategies)

Try to note each occasion as the day progresses rather than record all events at the end of the day.

3. Re-read your ccmpleted diary from Exercise 2. With the benefit of hindsight, suggest in column 5 ('alternative coping strategies') other ways you might have handled the situation.

4. Seek out and compile a list of welfare and counselling services and other resources available to nurses both locally and nationally. Be prepared to use them!

These may be run by statutory bodies such as the local health authority or local council, or by other bodies such as private charities. Organisations such as the Citizens' Advice Bureau or the Community Health Council may be able to help. To start you off:

- *Royal College of Nursing* CHAT (Counselling Help Advice Together): a confidential counselling service for all nurses. Telephone: 01–629 3870 or 01–409 3333.

Further Reading

Bond M (1986) *Stress and Self-awareness – A Guide to Nurses.* London: Heinemann.

Consumers Association (1982) *Living with Stress.* London: Consumers Association.

Lackman V D (1983) *Stress Management – A Manual for Nurses.* New York: Grune and Stratton.

Menzies I E P (1960) *A Case Study in the Functioning of Social Systems as a Defence Against Anxiety.* London: Tavistock Institute of Human Relations.

11
Managing Time

This chapter aims to introduce you to:

- The things which can affect time management on your unit
- A way of reviewing the way in which you and your staff use time
- A consideration of the purpose of ward reports related to the time they take
- Different ways of planning duty rotas

A feeling of pressure and not enough time to do things as one would wish are common enough; indeed, these are some of the reasons which people give for leaving nursing and seeking other occupations (Cunningham, 1980). These feelings arise regardless cf the fact that there has been a steady increase in the number of nurses working in the United Kingdom over the past twc decades. However, there has also been a sharp increase in the dependency of the patients they care for, partly as a result of much shorter stays in hospital. Coupled with this is the fact that the hours in an average working week have decreased, and holiday allowances have gone up (Moores, 1987), so there are few nurses who do not feel the consequences of such a situation (Figure 11.1).

Time is a precious resource and has to be managed well since once it has passed it has gone for ever. If we wish to join the battle of fighting for more resources or arguing for a decrease in workload, we have to be absolutely certain that the time that is available is well used, so it is worth sitting back for a while in order to consider how time is used in a clinical unit and to ask whether there is any way in which it could be used more effectively.

Several broad helping categories can be identified when considering the management of time, although it is difficult sometimes to identify these within one's own situation since it can create a feeling of discomfort if the established way of things has to be challenged. Yet it is a challenge that most of us have had to face at some point in our careers and which, once tackled, can lead to a much more peaceful life.

PROACTIVE v REACTIVE WORK

Many nurses pride themselves on being able to react well in an emergency or to respond to situations as they arise. Indeed, a great deal of nursing work requires this type of 'reactive' response as changes occur in clinical or organisational circumstances. Thus, every time something 'crops up', it is responded to on the spot. While this can be very necessary in some clinical situations, there are times when reactive responses can lead to poor use of time and result in a delay in important work because time has been spent in responding to the immediately visible situation.

Fig 11.1 I'm late, I'm late for a very important date

For example, some nurses feel a great urgency to 'get on with the work' when they come on duty in the morning and rush in, reacting to patients' needs as they can see them. One of two consequences can arise in this situation. First, there may be a terrible rush at the end of the shift because things have come to light which should have been done earlier in the day. Time may well have been spent in less important work which was immediately visible, but in a reactive approach this would not be evident until it was too late.

Alternatively, all work may (on rare occasions) be finished early when, in fact, the time was available to let a patient have an extra soak in the bath or to watch dressing techniques with the occupational therapist in order that the same pattern can be followed for that patient at a later date. Either way, 'getting on with the work' with no planning has its problems.

In a proactive approach a different pattern arises. All the work which needs to be undertaken is considered beforehand and a rough time plan made. Priorities can be set so that responses are made, not just to work which is immediately visible, but also to less obvious but equally important work. For example, a choice may have to be made between washing one patient's hair or spending time planning for discharge with another. While the first task is both visible and rewarding, the consequences of omitting the second are far greater. Sadly, priority decision-making of this kind does have to be made. What is important is that one can go home at the end of the day saying, 'I've made the right choices' when there just is not enough time to do everything.

A proactive approach also implies forward planning and allocating time to some activities which may not be immediately essential for day-to-day survival but are, nevertheless, very important aspects of productive work. For example, time set aside for team meetings, staff performance review, discussions with other members of the clinical team and so forth, is time well spent. This is just the sort of thing which can go 'overboard' in busy moments because it is not valued in the same way as other activities. Yet one of the biggest cries in many nurses' lives is the difficulty experienced in keeping communication channels open. Establishing effective communication networks, placing value on maintaining them and, except in dire emergencies, ensuring that the allocated time is protected, all become essential features of a well-run unit.

There are many other situations where a proactive approach to work can be timesaving, for example, making appointments with relatives when one knows one will not be too busy can save time for both parties. There is nothing worse than feeling the pressure of having to stop what one is doing to talk to relatives or of keeping them waiting, knowing that they are anxious and worried. Furthermore, unless plans are made, they can easily slip away unseen, so that further precious time can be lost in trying to contact them prior to, for example, discharge arrangements.

THE RIGHT PERSON FOR THE RIGHT JOB

Another timesaving mechanism which can be employed is ensuring that the right person is allocated to the right job, that is, within his or her capacity (see Chapter 3). If work is allocated to someone who is uncertain of the outcome, constant reference has to be made back to the senior nurse on duty. Alternatively, important signs of change may pass unnoticed through lack of understanding of their significance.

However, once work has been allocated it is equally important that the worker should be trusted to manage independently without being continuously checked on. Provided it is known that help or advice can be sought if necessary, people generally work much better if given the freedom and room to manage themselves. Giving people specific responsibility for some aspects of ward maintenance can also save time in the long run; for example, if someone is made responsible for ensuring that the equipment cupboard is always stocked, it will usually be well maintained. While it is certainly the senior nurse's responsibility to identify the stock items and set the levels required, it does not take years of nurse training and experience to maintain them. Once established, this is an example of work which could well be undertaken by an unqualified member of the ward team.

So a review of 'who does what' can be undertaken, posing several questions in relation to each area of work under consideration:

- What knowledge and skill are required to undertake this work?
- Which members of the team have these abilities?
- Are guidelines required to ensure the work is carried out as required?

Using senior nursing staff to carry out unskilled work is both costly and inefficient, and is difficult to justify to a general manager. While it is often easier in the short term to do something oneself, spending a little time ensuring that the right person is given guidance in order to be able to do the right work is, in the long run, much more efficient.

AVOIDANCE

It is very easy to fill one's day with things one likes doing, to the cost of things which are less enjoyable but nevertheless important. Many times one hears people saying, 'Oh, she's a good sister. She rolls up her sleeves and gets on with the nursing'. While this may be admirable in some circumstances, sisters and charge nurses have responsibilities within their job which are different from those of a staff nurse. If 'rolling up her sleeves' means that other work does not get done, the appropriateness of this sort of behaviour has to be questioned. Understandably, most nurses enjoy giving direct patient care and there are times when this is just what is needed, but time must also be set aside to 'manage' the ward, to plan, to negotiate, to teach and to help junior staff to develop.

Avoidance of work we do not like doing, by filling our time with other activities, is a very common behaviour. As I sit here writing my eye is on the windows, which need cleaning, and the lawn which needs cutting (both easier tasks than this!). It will be interesting to see which wins at the end of the day. While this may sound trivial, it is something we all need to examine in our own approach to work and question whether our own skills and those of others are being used to the best advantage at all times.

WARD REPORTS

Much time is spent by nurses in hand-over reports at different times of the day. Since they do occupy so much time, it is important to look at the value of this activity in order to see if it is always productive. For example, if five nurses listen to one half-hour report given by the night nurse, three hours of nursing time has been used before the day's work is begun. There are several questions which can be raised about ward reports to see if this is, in fact, the best way to spend that time.

What is the purpose of the ward report? Is it to say what has been done, to report any changes, or to say what still needs to be done? In other words, is the report 'descriptive' or 'prescriptive'? If a descriptive report is given, one has to question how much detail is actually required and how much crossover there is with written information and evaluation. For instance, while it may be very rewarding to tell people how you have spent your time over the past few hours, what is really important is the progress which the patients have made and any changes which have occurred. Thus descriptions of patient outcomes rather than just nursing actions become relevant.

Regarding the *prescriptive* component of reports, many nurses spend time giving detailed directions on the care which a patient will require during the next shift. This raises several questions: Who requires such detailed information? How well can it be retained when given verbally? What is the risk of misunderstanding when giving verbal instructions? Why repeat information if it is already written on the care plan? Care plans have not been widely accepted in the United Kingdom, with many excuses being made such as their being too time-consuming or never referred to. But, if we continue to use verbal reports in the traditional way, as a means of prescribing care, it is not surprising that they are not referred to, since the same work is being done twice. The question that has to be asked is, which is the better method? Knowing the frailty of human memory and the ease with which words can be misheard or misinterpreted, there seems little doubt that written care plans far outweigh a verbal prescription in terms of accuracy, consistency and, hence, safety.

Who should attend reports? Old habits die hard and it is difficult to convince nurses that they do not need detailed information about all patients on the unit. Yet if a system of primary nursing, team nursing or patient allocation is used the need for such a practice must be questioned. Surely it is better to know well a few patients for whom one will have responsibility, rather than all patients superficially. It takes an extremely exceptional person to be able to remember all the clinical details, yet alone the psychosocial background, of all patients, but this is what we commonly demand of ourselves.

However, suggesting that it is unnecessary for all nurses to know all patients often creates a feeling of insecurity amongst the staff. The cry of, 'What if there is an emergency?' is heard all too often. In reality this kind of situation rarely happens. If a nurse leaves the unit for a coffee break she can quickly highlight any points of concern to a colleague before she leaves. If an emergency does arise it is unlikely that the nurses who are not responsible for that patient's care will be able to recall the information given at report anyway, especially at a time of stress. So much of the felt need for all nurses to know about all patients is more to do with the way nurses feel than the way patients are nursed. Whether or not this is a justifiable use of time is open to debate.

It is also worth while mentioning here that for a written communication, with both descriptive and prescriptive components, to be effective, it must be easily available to the staff requiring it and not tucked away in some inaccessible place. If it is kept in a filing cabinet or an office, an extra effort has to be made to leave patients to seek out the information, with the result that reference is rarely made to it, thus reducing its impact.

TEACHING AND COMMUNICATION TIME

Two things which nurses often say they do not have the time for are teaching and ward meetings, both important aspects of ward work. If the traditional use of time spent at ward reports is challenged, it is one way of freeing time for these other functions. Thus, an opportunity can be made for nursing care conferences about either a particular patient's nursing needs or a particular nursing problem. Standards of care may be discussed or plans made for development, all those things which get left out because of lack of time. It is certainly worth thinking about.

PRIORITY SETTING

Some mention has already been made of priority setting but it is such an important issue that it is worth raising again. Unfortunately, in virtually any work situation there are times when it is impossible to do everything that one would wish, so decisions have to be made about what must be done first and what must be left until later. It is very easy to respond to situations as they arise rather than plan logically and few nurses will not recognise the feeling of one of those days when everyone wants something at once.

One approach to priority setting is to classify work, once it has been identified, into two basic classes – those things which *must* be done because they are essential to life, and those things which you *want* to be able to achieve which contribute to the quality of life. Using a hierarchy of needs, such as the one described by Maslow (1954), can be helpful in differentiating between the two, although it is not a rigid structure which must be followed at all times. Maslow classified needs in a pyramidal shape (Figure 11.2) and suggested that until lower-order needs had been met people were unconcerned about higher-order needs.

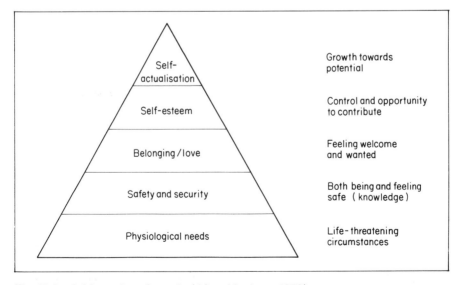

Fig 11.2 A hierarchy of needs (After Maslow, 1970)

Thus, when setting priorities, physiological needs which may be life-threatening, such as the need for air and food, take precedence. This does not, however, suggest that some of the other physical needs such as hygiene would have to be placed so highly. Following these are needs for safety and security which, it can be suggested, are closely related to knowing what is happening. Ensuring that people have sufficient information to understand their circumstances, know what will be happening to them and when it will occur are therefore placed high on a list of priorities. In simple terms, this may be letting someone know the time of an impending X-ray rather than just saying that it will be at some time during the day. At a more complex level, it may mean giving people time to ask questions about their future. Belonging and feeling needed and loved come next, which at a clinical level may be the manner in which people are approached. Self-esteem, through some control over what happens, is the need next in order and, finally, self-actualisation or reaching of potential.

It must be stressed, however, that this hierarchy does not follow at all times for there are those who would reverse the order in some circumstances. Thus, the most important thing for one person may be to retain control in order to preserve self-esteem, even if a physiological risk is involved. The hierarchy can only act as a starting guide and should never be used without assessing each situation at an individual level.

PLANNING DUTY ROTAS

Planning the duty rota is not a job which many nurses are fond of, but there are some ways in which it can be made less burdensome. As a starting point, it is essential to have a series of basic, realistic *guidelines* relating to the factors which will influence the safe provision of nursing, which all the staff are familiar with, and which are planned within the ward budget. Points which will influence the guidelines are outlined below.

Pattern of Work

Some units can predict fluctuations in the pattern of work throughout the week according to such things as operating days or emergency admission days. Other units are less affected by such factors and, indeed, it may be that the nursing workload actually increases at the weekend when team members from other disciplines are less readily available. In the same way, peaks and troughs may occur throughout the day. Good planning can very often smooth the peaks and troughs, for example, by offering people the opportunity to bath at different times of the day, or organising patient teaching for less busy moments, but in some circumstances they are unavoidable. For instance, if many patients need help with their eating and drinking, meal times can then become busy. Mapping out a pattern of predictable changes in workload is an essential beginning stage to planning duty rotas.

Staff Available

One of the advantages of undertaking a job analysis (discussed in Chapter 2) is that it acts as a guide to deciding which type of staff is most suitable in each clinical setting. With these points in mind, it is possible to review the allocation of staff to a unit and question whether it is appropriate. In many situations, allocations were made a long time ago, and with alterations in the dependency of the patients arising from a faster throughput the situation may well have changed. It is worth bearing in mind that the *quantity* of staff is sometimes less important than the *quality* of people's professional skills. For example, if an unqualified member cf the ward team is placed in a situation where changes occur very rapidly, she will have to refer back to a qualified team member at frequent intervals; this is both time-consuming and frustrating. In this sort of situation it may be better to reduce the actual number of people available but increase the requirement for professional qualifications. With an understanding of the budget allocated to each clinical unit for staffing and the equivalence in terms of hours of changing one grade of staff for another, senior clinical nurses can make adjustments of this kind in order to meet the needs of their own specific clinical environment.

Hours

We often become locked within fixed duty hours which have been arranged at a hospital or unit level, yet the pattern of work in different units often varies widely so that nurses are forced into a situation of trying to make individual care plans for patients which fit into set nursing hours. Provided that the correct number of hours has been worked by the time it comes to pay-day there is no reason why such a rigid approach has to be taken.

Prior to the days of primary nursing, patient allocation or care planning, staff arriving at different times of day was difficult to cope with. It meant that extra time had to be taken giving reports on all patients and it was difficult to know how well the work was progressing. However, the advent of these things allows for a much more flexible approach to timing, which can have great advantages; for instance, a primary nurse may consider it appropriate to come on duty later than usual in the morning, knowing that she will be able to stay late with one of her patients who will be returning from theatre.

Another advantage of flexibility in hours is that there is a greater chance of being able to accommodate part-time staff who are unable to work some of the set shift patterns. At a time when it is difficult in many areas to find sufficient staff, this has to be taken into consideration. Similarly, job-sharing may be another way around finding appropriate cover, where two people are able between them to work the hours needed, provided they have the flexibility to arrange their share themselves.

Even though flexibility is strongly recommended, there do still have to be some basic ground rules about the minimum cover needed for safety and other requirements. These may include:

- The number of registered nurses required on each shift throughout the week; this will obviously vary according to the shifting workload and the time of day
- The minimum number of *people* required on each shift
- The times when it is essential to be present and the times when it is possible to be flexible; for example, one person would have to be responsible for taking over from the night staff each morning
- Agreement about the number of weekend and evening shifts that each person will cover
- Personal preferences, where possible, to allow for attending night classes, etc.
- Allowance for team meetings, either with the primary nurses' team or the whole ward team
- Allowance for multidisciplinary meetings, ward rounds and policy meetings
- The number of weekend/evening duties expected of each team member

If at all possible, the sister or charge nurse should not be included in the duty rota as part of the essential cover since the role is different from that of the other team members. Whoever occupies this role should have sufficient flexibility to be able to work hours which enable him or her to fulfil the managerial as well as the clinical components of the role.

However, it is not always possible to achieve this desirable situation, in which case a compromise may have to be made, with specific hours or days designated to clinical work and others to managerial work. Some have achieved this by carrying a very small case-load as a primary nurse, thus doing some clinical work each day but also allocating time to teaching, managing and planning. Others have whole days allocated to different components of the work. Whichever approach is taken, the important thing is to recognise the variety of work and ensure that time is allocated for each component.

Once these basic principles have been worked through, several different approaches to planning the duty rota can be taken. These include fixed rotas, rotas planned by staff and 'flexihours'.

Fixed Rotas

A pattern of duties can be prepared for a period of between four and six weeks which 'repeats' itself throughout the year. The great advantage of this is that it largely does away with the need for a request book because rather than having to plan the duty rota around requests, staff are in a position to organise their personal lives, knowing well ahead which weekends and evenings will be free. If a special event such as a wedding falls on a working week-end, the person can negotiate with a colleague, well in advance, to swap duties. Plans to visit friends or have a week-end away can be arranged to fit in with free time.

At first sight, some people will resist the fixed rota approach since they fear it will restrict their time. However, once the system is established people are usually reluctant to return to old ways, for the advantages are great. There is security in knowing when free time is available, and the worry of not knowing whether a request will be granted is removed.

Even with fixed rotas, there is plenty of room for flexibility. It is possible to indicate on the rota who is responsible for co-ordinating the ward on each shift and therefore has to be available at specific hours. However, on other days hours can be adjusted to meet different patient needs provided that the minimum requirements for safety are met.

Rotas Planned By the Staff

Another way of handling duty rotas is for the staff to plan their own hours of work. Once the basic guidelines have been established and a skeleton for essential cover prepared, staff can fill in their own duties within the framework. This approach can be very helpful in creating team cohesiveness and recognition of responsibility.

Flexihours

Because it is so difficult to predict the workload in many wards, some places have introduced the idea of flexihours where staff can adjust their working time according to the fluctuations in workload. For example, if extra staffing has been planned to cover the morning after an emergency 'take' night when in fact there were few admissions, staff are in a position to adjust their duties, thus freeing time to put in extra work when the ward is very busy. Of course, care has to be taken not to take advantage of those who are always willing to alter their plans in this sort of situation, but provided there is trust and mutual respect within the team the system can work very well and the hours can be 'evened out' by the end of the month.

When working with people in a clinical situation there is always something to be done and rarely enough time for everything. Yet it is easy to get into the 'habit' of being busy. Good management of time does ensure the best use of the time that is available and avoids the trap of doing things in a certain way from habit and routine rather than because they are the most important. Time spent in planning and priority setting is well worth it in the long run and will, at least, contribute to eliminating that terrible feeling of not getting through everything, and allow the nurse to go home at the end of the day feeling that a good job has been done.

EXERCISES

1. By counting the number of people attending ward reports and the length of time spent during reports over a day, calculate how much nursing time is spent in this activity.

2. Over a three-day period, make a note of the type of information shared at report. How much is:

- A description of what nurses have done?
- Information about how patients have responded?
- Prescriptions of what needs to be done?
- Discussion about clinical problems or interests?

Make a note of any other places where each of these areas of information may be repeated, such as in patients' progress notes or care plans.

3. If you do not have regular ward meetings for staff, consider whether these would be beneficial. Describe:

- How you would prepare an agenda for a ward meeting (see Chapter 5)
- Who would be responsible for recording what happened
- How you would ensure that all team members would know what had been discussed
- What time would be most convenient for holding such meetings

4. Review your duty rota and identify the criteria which are used as guidelines when it is prepared. If these are not clear, identify the minimum requirements for safe cover. Could the duty rota be an agenda item for your team meeting?

Further Reading

Ford R D (ed.) (1982) *1000 Nursing Tips and Time Savers*. London: Baillière Tindall/Springhouse Publishing Co.

Lakein A (1979) *How to Get Control of Your Time and Life*. Aldershot: Gower Publishing.

Maslow A H (1954) *Motivation and Personality*. New York: Harper and Row.

Matthews A (1982) *In Charge of the Ward*. Oxford: Blackwell Scientific Publications.

Rowden R (1984) *Managing Nursing: A Practical Introduction to Management for Nurses*. London: Baillière Tindall.

Walton M (1984) *Management and Managing – A Dynamic Approach*. London: Harper and Row.

12
Standards

The purpose of this chapter is to:

- Clarify what is meant by 'standards'
- Discuss the need to identify standards
- Examine how standards may be set in a clinical environment

Currently, there is much discussion and publicity about standards. Nurses talk about the difficulty of maintaining standards, the problems of falling standards and the need for high standards. It would appear that many nurses also have difficulty in clarifying exactly what is meant by these statements as these are vague, subjective judgments which, for the most part, cannot be substantiated. There is a need, therefore, to:

- Define the term 'standard'
- Establish the need for standards
- Clarify the relationship of standards to the quality of the nursing service
- Examine the setting and monitoring of standards

CLARIFICATION OF THE TERM 'STANDARD'

A standard is a statement of a defined level of quality or competence which is expected in a given set of circumstances. In nursing, the statements identify and define the criteria which influence the quality or competence of the nursing service and say, in each case, what is expected. For example, it can be suggested that the nature of the nurse–patient relationship is an important criterion which influences the quality of nursing. In this case a standard describing the kind of relationship which is expected would have to be made, such as the degree of choice the nurse offers the patient when planning care. Thus a criterion is merely the name of the component which is being considered, while the standard is a description of the actual behaviour expected (Bloch, 1977). It is worth noting here that the criteria identified are often complex in nature and usually require that a number of separate standards be defined for each one.

For each criterion which is identified, standards may be considered in three main categories, namely those which are concerned with:

- structure,
- process
- outcome

Standards either make reference to the organisational factors which are influential (structure criteria), to the method by which things are to be done (process criteria) or to the outcomes to be achieved (outcome criteria). For example, taking the common clinical activity of giving a bed pan, there are structural criteria, such as the availability of equipment, process criteria, such as the manner in which the bed pan is offered, and outcome criteria, such as the time delay between the request and the service, all of which influence the quality of the actual procedure. Figure 12.1 shows an example of how these components may be summarised.

| | Activity – Giving a bed pan | | |
	Structure	Process	Outcome
Criteria	Availability of equipment	Privacy Technique	Response to request
Standard	2 slipper pans 10 pan holders Constant supply of 'liners'	Curtains always used Quiet conversation Positioned comfortably	All requests responded to in less than 2 minutes

Fig 12.1 Structure, process and outcome standards

Thus for each procedure or discrete situation, criteria which relate to structure, process and outcome can be identified and a minimum standard which could be expected can be agreed upon. Within these categories, both qualitative and quantitive standards can be identified. Clarification of the standards expected also has implications for the evaluation of care and for performance review (see Chapter 7).

THE NEED FOR STANDARDS

Demands are being made by society for a quality service which will cater for a wide variety of health-care needs. The deliberate setting of standards allows for identification and clarification of those factors which are considered to be essential components of a competent nursing service. The desire to achieve the described components then becomes the force directing nursing practice. The description of each standard also represents the desired situation against which comparisons can be made. This makes deliberate and substantiated evaluation possible by those responsible and accountable for nursing and may indicate when and where change is necessary.

Without clearly-defined standards it is impossible to say whether or not the service which is offered is acceptable to either clients or those who are responsible for its maintenance. If the factors which are acceptable to both of these groups have not been clarified, it is very difficult to give reasons for asking for more resources or a reduction in the workload in times of pressure. Furthermore, if people are unclear about the standard which is expected of them, they are working in a vacuum. How can they work to an agreed level of performance if these expectations are not made clear?

However, it is also worthy of note that, if standards are set too tightly, they can inhibit the development of the service. The degree of precision to which the activity is described is largely dependent on the ability of the carer. Thus, when working with unqualified carers it may be necessary to break each activity into fairly detailed components in order to ensure that the required standard is fully understood. In contrast, experienced staff need some room to exercise their discretion in the way in which they nurse, and may be constrained if the standards which have been described do not leave them such a degree of freedom.

THE RELATIONSHIP OF STANDARDS TO A QUALITY SERVICE

Standard setting can help to ensure a quality service in the following two ways:

- By the identification of those criteria which influence the quality or competence of the service
- By the detailed description of the criteria in order that comparisons can be made of what is desirable against what has been achieved (i.e. evaluation); this provides information about

the state of the service and where adjustments, if any, need to be made

The criteria which are identified as being important are, to a large extent, influenced by the ideology or beliefs of the people concerned, and it must be remembered that if people have different beliefs they will also have different standards which are important to them. Thus, if nursing is merely viewed as an adjunct to medicine, the criteria will focus on such things as the fulfilment of medical prescription and the management of the disease process, and these components become all important. However, if nursing is seen as a separate but complementary occupational group with a clearly-defined, independent function such as helping people to be independent, to adapt to stresses which affect them or to achieve the ability to care for themselves, different standards will be viewed as being essential to the provision of a quality service.

A prerequisite to setting standards is, therefore, the identification of the value system from which one practises. Without an agreement of this kind, it is possible that conflict can occur, since there may be a difference of opinion as to what constitutes good nursing. This can be seen both amongst nurses themselves and in their relationship with other occupational groups. For example, if one nurse believes that her function is solely concerned with the physiological safety of the patient, she will not be concerned with standards which relate to sociological issues such as family involvement; moreover, she may become irritated by the nurse who takes time to deal with this component of work. In the same way, there can be a variance of opinion between nurses and other health-care workers if both the value system and standards are not made clear.

SETTING AND MONITORING STANDARDS

In the setting and monitoring of standards, the following areas can be identified for discussion:

- The 'ingredients' of nursing
- The 'method' of nursing (a systematic approach)
- Audit or nursing evaluation
- Client satisfaction

The 'Ingredients' of Nursing

A philosophy of care or the conceptualisation of nursing results in the identification and clarification of those 'ingredients' which are seen to be important and valued (people, their environments, health and nursing – see Chapter 2), and these form the basis from which the majority of standards are formulated. For example, one important belief which must be clarified is how people are viewed. They may be seen as 'biological creatures subject to disease' (medical model) or it may be agreed that each person is unique and individual. This will obviously influence many aspects of the nursing service such as the data-collecting activity related to assessment. If the first view is taken, only data concerned with the disease process will then be required and, if this is present, the standard would be met. However, if a fuller view is taken, data about other aspects of life would be expected and, if the assessment was confined to biological information alone, this would constitute unacceptable practice. Returning to the earlier classification, criteria related to each of the three components can be seen in Figure 12.2.

	Structure	Process	Outcome
Criteria	Recording document	Relationship	Content
Standard	Sufficient room to record all information in an easily retrievable form	Opportunity for patient to express his or her views	Evidence of physical, social and psychological data, in appropriate proportions

Fig 12.2   Criteria in each area

However, standards may also emerge as a result of legislation, local policy and public demand. For example, every nurse must attend a fire lecture annually, must have undertaken a recognised course in order to be entitled to call him or herself a nurse and have breaks from duty after an agreed number of hours.

Systematic Approach to Care

The method of nursing most widely acknowledged at present is a systematic approach based upon the action research model. This method is, in itself, a standard which may be looked for when approval is being sought for courses which lead to a statutory qualification. One of the reasons for such a decision is that, by the nature of the activities encompassed within this method, it allows for the setting and subsequent monitoring of standards on

a day-to-day basis for individual clients in each unique setting
(the nursing process, see Part I, Chapter 2).

The activities of the systematic approach to care which particularly relate to the setting and monitoring of standards are the
identification of goals or objectives and analysis and evaluation
of outcomes. Goal-setting is concerned with the identification of
the desired outcomes for the individual patient or client and these
are the standards which it is hoped will be met by that person in
his or her unique situation. The quality of the nursing service can
be judged by the frequency with which clients are able to reach
their personalised gcals or the standards which have been set
with them on an individual basis, through the implementation cf
the prescribed nursing. Deliberate evaluation by the nurse and
client allows decisions to be made regarding the success or failure
in meeting the standard which has been agreed for that particular
client in his unique setting.

These points stress the importance of setting realistic goals with
clients. However, monitoring standards can also act as an early
warning system if, for example, one particular goal is not met,
giving an opportunity to investigate at an early point why this is
so. Similarly, it may be possible to see whether organisational
factors such as a staff shortage have an adverse effect on agreed
standards, and give weight to discussions on this subject.

Audit or Nursing Evaluation

Over the last few years the term audit has crept into the nursing
vocabulary; for many nurses the word creates a feeling of unease
and suspicion. In the light of these feelings, it is worth while
exploring the nature and function of the nursing audit, or
evaluation as some people prefer to call it.

A nursing audit or evaluation is the calling of the individual
nurse or the clinical nursing unit to account for the care delivered.
What is paramount here is the adjective attached to the word
audit, namely 'nursing'. A nursing audit is a tool designed by
nurses, to be used by nurses, in the self-assessment and evaluation
of the service which they offer. As professionals it is both
right and proper that nurses should account and, therefore, be
accountable for the service they provide.

It is worth while noting here that the use of the word audit has
become synonymous with the once or twice-yearly overall review
of the nursing service and is used in this context here. However,
technically the day-to-day concurrent review, as discussed earlier
in relation to the nursing process, could be referred to as an audit.

In some instances, organisational managers have imposed an auditing system which has, on rare occasions, been known to be used punitively. However, in other organisations, units will request audit personally in order to use the information as a basis for planning and development and this is the approach which relates to the situation described above.

An audit is dependent upon the prior determination of standards. It is important to note that the setting of standards is not part of the audit process itself. The audit involves the assessment and evaluation of the nurse or clinical nursing unit in relation to the standards which have been predetermined by a body such as a standards committee. Audit also allows for continuous assessment and evaluation of the standard itself in order to be sure that it is both reasonable and achievable. Communication of the findings of clinical audits to the standards committee helps them to identify any discrepancies, so that changes can be made where appropriate. For example, one criterion which may have been considered by the standards committee is that of postoperative infection rates, with standards outlined as shown in Figure 12.3.

	Structure	Process	Outcome
Criteria	Materials	Wound management	Percentage of infected wounds
Standard	Constant provision of dressing packs	Aseptic dressing technique	Less than 2 per cent per annum

Fig 12.3 Postoperative infection rates

Let us suppose here that the audit has shown a 10 per cent rise in the rate, and that subsequently the rate has risen to 12 per cent despite the structure standards and process standards having been met. This means that all three criteria must be re-examined to see if they were realistic and the possibility that other factors were influencing the outcome must be investigated. It may be that there is a source of infection in theatre, that a member of the team is a 'carrier' and needs treatment or that there has been a change in the client group receiving care to one that is more susceptible to infection. What is important is that the discrepancy has been identified and can be investigated.

Audits can be carried out concurrently or retrospectively. A concurrent audit evaluates a situation where nursing care is currently being given – the client is still being nursed within the care system, not yet having been discharged. With this approach, it is possible to look at either the process of nursing, that is the care as it is actually being given, or the outcome of nursing, that is, the response of the client. Obviously, the most desirable position is one where the process can be directly linked to the outcome. Some evidence is now becoming available for this purpose, such as the known association of preoperative information to the degree of postoperative pain (Hayward, 1975) but, up to now, most predesigned audit tools have concentrated on one aspect or another, presuming an association.

A retrospective audit, on the other hand, evaluates the care given solely from the nursing records and, in this case, the client may no longer be in the care system. It is unfortunate that the majority of nursing records are insufficient to provide enough information to be of any great value, but many units have made great strides in managing their nursing records in recent years and the position is gradually improving. Again, with this system, an assumption is made that the records reflect the actual care given.

As with most tools, there are both advantages and disadvantages to concurrent and retrospective auditing but insufficient data are available at present on which to judge whether one or the other provides the most useful information. It would appear that a combination of both concurrent and retrospective approaches could give the most accurate picture of the actual situation and it can be suggested that this combined approach should be adopted. However, it should also be noted that as the retrospective audit is completely dependent upon the availability of accurate nursing records, its use may still be limited in many situations.

The evaluation is normally recorded by means of a scoring system, devised by the audit committee; this allows it to be compared with the standards identified by the standards committee.

There are a number of audit packages which have been developed, primarily in the USA, specifically for use by nurses and which are readily available. However, two such packages have been used relatively widely in the United Kingdom. 'Monitor' (Goldstone et al, 1983) has been modified and adapted from the Rush Medicus system for use in the UK, and versions relating to acute general nursing, district nursing and mental health nursing are now available. Initially, Monitor requires that patients are placed in one of four dependency categories; a number of patients from each category is then selected and a series of questions posed, the answers being taken from several different sources including records, observation and by asking the patient or nurse. In each case the answer is limited to, 'Yes', 'No' or 'Not Applicable'. There is also a ward-based questionnaire seeking information about the way in which the ward is organised. Monitor provides a highly structured approach to audit; however, there is little room for professional judgment and, consequently, a risk that those who are most creative in their approach to nursing might not score well as they do not work within the parameters of the assessment tool.

The second system which has been used quite widely is known as QUALPAC (Wandelt et al, 1974). This system looks at the process of nursing concurrently, that is, while it is actually happening. It consists of a 68-item scale subdivided into six sections concerned with:

1. *Psychosocial – individual*   Actions directed towards meeting the psychosocial needs of patients
2. *Psychosocial – group*   Actions directed towards meeting the psychosocial needs of patients as members of a group
3. *Physical*   Actions directed towards meeting the physical needs of patients
4. *General*   Actions directed towards meeting either psychosocial or physical needs of the patient, or both at the same time
5. *Communication*   Communication on behalf of the patient
6. *Professional implications*   Care given to patients reflects initiative and responsibility indicative of professional expectations

Scoring is on a scale of 1 (poorest care) to 5 (best care). A series of cues is supplied as examples of how the scoring may be applied but, before using the scale, assessors usually attend a workshop to work through the system and look for professional agreement as to how each item should be scored. While this system is also limited to the predefined items, it does provide more flexibility in both allowing for professional judgment and in scaling the scoring. Some people have criticised QUALPAC as being too 'woolly', but it has been used very successfully by clinical nurses in some districts as a 'diagnostic tool', giving them some sort of measure whereby they can plan change and evaluate the progress they have made.

The use of predesigned tools can be very helpful to practitioners. Nevertheless, if an audit is to have meaning, it is sometimes more appropriate to design a protocol for each individual clinical unit which can be used in conjunction with the predesigned tools. This proposal is based on the fact that the audit package contains some criteria to be evaluated which may not coincide with the local situation. Furthermore, there may well be criteria which are highly relevant at a local level but not appropriate to a wider audience. For example, the client population in one area may be multiracial and standards would have to be set which relate to the provision of facilities which will suit their particular circumstances; this may not be the case in another area and those standards would be redundant.

A substantial initiative is required to prepare an auditing tool which is appropriate to each setting and sensitive to the particular situation in which it will be used. Nevertheless, it is recognised that some elements of an audit package will be common to all auditing situations and they can be a very valuable starting point.

In the light of this proposal there is a need for the formation of local nursing standards and auditing committees, which can accept the responsibility for setting standards and providing an auditing service for clinical nurses.

Client Satisfaction

With personalised care there is a need to take into consideration the opinions of the consumer or client just as would be done in the retail or catering industries. Client satisfaction can be monitored in three ways:

- First, on a day-to-day basis by evaluation of patient outcomes
- Second, by the identification of items contained in the once- or twice-yearly overall audit which can be assessed and evaluated by the client
- Third, by the completion of a separately-designed questionnaire which will be completed by the client as part of a specific exercise to determine client satisfaction (Wright, 1987)

This can prove to be a very difficult exercise because many clients are either unable or unwilling to criticise the nursing service: it has been suggested that some patients may fear reprisals if they voice their criticisms. Furthermore, it is very difficult to make a judgment if one does not know what alternatives are available; for example, some patients may think that it is impossible to adjust their waking hour and so will say that an early start to the day is an acceptable standard. Similarly, they may not know of alternative ways in which assistance can be given to help them to dress independently and thus accept a service which some nurses would consider to be unacceptable. This does not mean that their opinions should not be sought but that account must be taken of these factors when considering the standards which are identified for each unit.

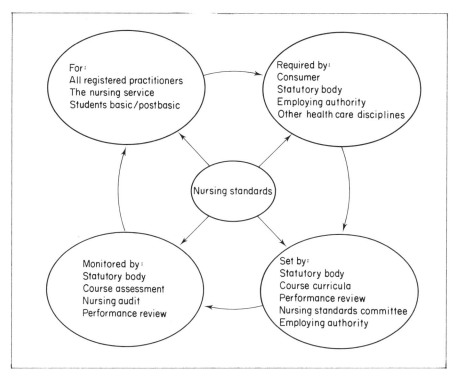

Fig 12.4   A summary of the factors that influence standards

Figure 12.4 summarises some of the issues which are related to setting standards. The implications are widespread for all nurses and a topic which must be addressed if we wish to account for the service we offer and to be sure that it is acceptable both to clients and to ourselves.

EXERCISES

1. Working from your unit philosophy (Chapter 6), identify three criteria you would consider important in relationship to assessment in your unit (e.g. data collected, etc.).

2. Identify the standards you would expect for each of these criteria (e.g. a balance between physical, social and psychological data).

3. Assess whether the standards you have identified are being met on your unit and, if not, see if you can establish where the problem lies (e.g. do your assessment forms show data relating to physical, social and psychological needs?).

4. Raise the issue of standards as an agenda item at your next unit meeting and discuss whether it would be appropriate to explore the similarities and variances of opinion about desirable standards within the team. It may also be useful to consider whether there is understanding between the nurses and other health-care workers about acceptable standards, but do remember that these must be realistic.

Further Reading

Kitson A (1988) Raising the standards. *Nursing Times*, **84**(25): 28–32.

Pearson A (ed.) (1987) *Nursing Quality Measurement: Quality Assurance Methods for Peer Review*. Chichester: HM+M/John Wiley and Sons.

Schroeder P and Marbusch R (1984) *Nursing Quality Assurance: A Unit-based Approach*. Rockville, MD: Aspen Publications.

13
Career Structures and Staff Support Roles

This chapter is concerned with:

- The nature of staff support services
- The way in which they may be used
- The role of clinical nurse specialists
- Relationships with other paramedical disciplines

Traditionally, nurses have worked in a bureaucratic structure which was formalised by the Salmon (DHSS, 1966) and Mayston (DHSS, 1969) reports. Within this setting there has been a strict pecking order, senior nurses spending much of their time in checking the activities of less experienced staff and ensuring that rules and regulations have been adhered to. There has, however, been a gradual shift away from this system of management to a much freer atmosphere and this must continue if nurses are expected to act as autonomous professional practitioners, working independently, using their professional judgment and exercising discretion in the way in which they do things. Obviously, there are basic principles relating to the overall goals of the organisation which have to be adhered to but, on the whole, the mood is much less restrictive than it has been in the past.

In the light of such changes, and in particular the manner in which nurses are striving to work, it can be seen that a bureaucratic line management structure is no longer appropriate. There is no place for a hierarchy concerned with clinical decision-making above the senior nurse practitioner. This leaves us with the need to review career options and their associated value systems within nursing in relation to the development of an appropriate nursing structure.

STRUCTURES

Until the Griffiths report (DHSS, 1983), nursing primarily associated career development with that of organisational management posts, to which both prestige and monetary rewards were linked. This has left other options for progress undervalued and, in many instances, unrecognised. Furthermore, the Griffiths recommendations clearly moved management posts into the arena of general management and, in the eyes of some, this has created a void in terms of career opportunities. An alternative view may be that it has created the opportunity for a 'real' career in management for those who deliberately choose to follow this path. From a positive perspective, it has also opened up the chance to reappraise other career options in nursing which have hitherto been stifled.

It has now been recognised that in the delivery of a nursing service there are essentially two groups of workers: one which actually nurses and the other which supports those giving the care. The support group includes those nurses with a personnel, administrative or educational function. Inherent in this kind of organisation is the belief that one group of workers is as important as the other in working towards a common goal, in this case the delivery of quality clinical nursing. The implication of this is that both the care givers and the supporters are of equal importance, which should be acknowledged in the structures, prestige and remunerative rewards.

It is important to point out that within each work group there is a hierarchical substructure which is based upon expertise, experience, qualifications and training or supervisory needs of the individuals concerned. However, recognition of the value of each function suggests the need to develop structures which are horizontal in their relationship and where different skills and knowledge are seen not in terms of one being superior to another but as complementing one another (Figure 13.1).

A Service

One of the results of changes of this kind has been the evolution of staff support posts in nursing. Essentially, the purpose of any staff support post is to provide a service to the practitioners, which is a fundamentally different function from the line management role we have worked with for so long.

The overall purpose of a hospital can be described as providing the best possible service for patients within the resources available. Thus it can be argued that the most crucial people within the organisation are those who provide clinical care directly, and that the function of all other personnel is to provide a service to the clinicians in order that they can be free to practise without worrying excessively about organisational issues. This does not mean to say that other roles are any less important, rather that

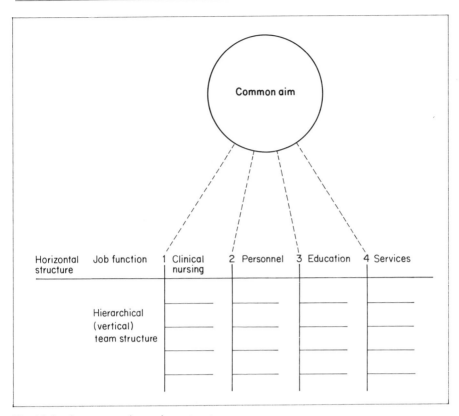

Fig 13.1 A proposed nursing structure

the relationship is interdependent, all working to a common goal of the actual provision of the clinical care.

The implications of this are that there is a change of relationship between nurses in different roles and that the perception that nurses in non-clinical roles are more senior does not necessarily hold water. What is important is that the service they supply is useful and appropriate to the needs of the clinical staff. If this premise is accepted, a clear responsibility can be seen for clinical staff in identifying the types of service which would be useful to them. There is no doubt that they are in the best position to be able to say what types of service are helpful in running a clinical unit and the way in which they would like access to them.

CAREER OPTIONS

It is possible to review career options in nursing in the light of both horizontal and hierarchical structuring, and some suggestions are given here. The discussion is centred around the groups identified previously, namely those who deliver care and those who provide a support service. Greater emphasis has been given to the latter group since it moves away from more traditional approaches. The options discussed are by no means exclusive and there are many others of differing nature which may be both appropriate and valuable.

Care Givers

Care givers are those who are directly responsible and hence accountable for the immediate delivery of nursing. Within this framework it is possible to consider a clinical career pattern which would be built on the appropriate expertise, experience, knowledge and skills of the practitioners in the particular area. One such structure is outlined in Figure 13.2.

Leading the team is the clinical nurse consultant, the expert who can be called upon to support other team members, who defines policy and standards for the unit and, possibly, has an added component within his or her realm of responsibility such as a specific responsibility for research or teaching of students.

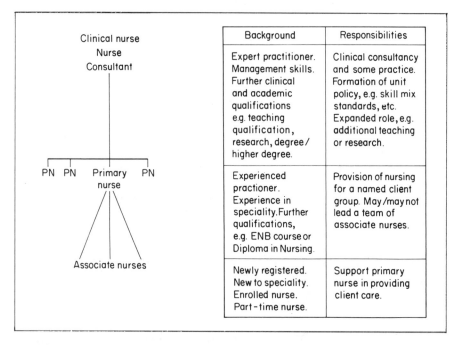

Background	Responsibilities
Expert practitioner. Management skills. Further clinical and academic qualifications e.g. teaching qualification, research, degree / higher degree.	Clinical consultancy and some practice. Formation of unit policy, e.g. skill mix standards, etc. Expanded role, e.g. additional teaching or research.
Experienced practioner. Experience in speciality. Further qualifications, e.g. ENB course or Diploma in Nursing.	Provision of nursing for a named client group. May /may not lead a team of associate nurses.
Newly registered. New to speciality. Enrolled nurse. Part-time nurse.	Support primary nurse in providing client care.

Clinical nurse
Nurse Consultant

PN PN Primary PN
nurse

Associate nurses

Fig 13.2 A clinical team structure

The primary nurse is an experienced clinical practitioner who takes responsibility for the nursing of a group of patients or clients within the framework established by the consultant. Other team members may be at various stages of career development, such as the newly qualified nurse or one who is new to the clinical speciality, but they work within the prescription of care devised by the primary nurse. Each post would be one with identified prerequisites, to which a named person is appointed.

Support Staff

The way in which staff support services can be developed is wide and varied. There are, however, some basic principles which can act as a guide in considering which ones may be of greatest value in different areas. These include consideration of:

- The provision of a service needed and valued by practitioners
- The ability to respond to the changing needs of practitioners
- Collegial relationships with those giving direct care
- Mutual respect between practitioners and those in staff support posts
- An opportunity to learn how to use staff support posts

It would be impossible to outline all the different staff support posts which could be developed as there are so many and they depend to a large extent on the services which are already available through other means. However, some are described below, giving consideration to the way in which they can gradually change over a period of time as nursing moves towards a professional model of practice.

Personnel Services

The classic description of personnel work identifies several major functions, including selection and appraisal of staff, clarification of both local and national policy, training, including statutory requirements such as fire regulations and safety procedures, career guidance and development, and relationships and communication. While all these functions have a very important place in any organisation, that of staff appointments is one which is particularly pertinent to nursing.

It has been the practice in many hospitals for personnel staff, alongside other nurse managers, to fulfil two major functions in relation to staffing. Firstly, they have controlled the mix of staff within a ward and decided how many registered nurses, enrolled nurses and auxiliaries should be employed within the limits of the budget. Secondly, they have processed applications, interviewed and appointed staff and then allocated them to a clinical unit.

However, in many places this practice is now changing. It is being recognised more and more widely that the most appropriate person to decide on the mix of skills required in a clinical team, within the allocated budget, is the manager/co-ordinator of that team, that is, the senior clinical nurse. He or she is also in the best position to be able to judge the sort of person who would fit into the ward team most comfortably, sharing the same values and being able to help to maintain the cohesiveness which is so essential for good working relationships. If this approach is taken, the function of the personnel nurse shifts from one of controlling staff mix and staff appointments to one of providing a service which helps the senior clinical nurse with staff appointments.

Many of the administrative tasks such as advertising, processing of forms, gathering references, and so forth, can be undertaken centrally. Similarly, advice and teaching can be offered on how to interview for appointment since this is a skill with which many nurses are unfamiliar. If people are unfamiliar with the procedure, advice can also be given on how to adjust staffing ratios, although the actual responsibility for appointing staff to work together lies with those with whom they will be working on a day-to-day basis.

Support Posts in Education

The provision of learning opportunities can be divided essentially into two broad categories. First, there is an area which can be described as 'in-service training' and which is concerned with such issues as orientation, fire lectures and resuscitation training, all of which are essential to the safety and smooth running of the service. It implies the provision of information and some skill training.

The use of the word 'training' has fallen into some disrepute amongst nurses in recent times. However, training implies bringing someone to 'a desired state or standard of proficiency' (Concise Oxford Dictionary, 1956) and this requirement cannot be ignored, especially in relation to some skills concerned with safety. Provision of training of this kind is essential to the smooth running of the unit and, indeed, lack of provision is indefensible since it can lead to potentially dangerous situations.

Second, there is a need for learning opportunities which will enhance the professional development of staff. In this instance, there is a shift from training about specific procedures to the provision of learning opportunities which facilitate the development of clinical practice. In many cases, it is the clinical staff themselves who can identify learning needs and request opportunities for particular experiences. Some units have developed the idea of 'learning contracts' (Keyser, 1986) where a facilitator and a practitioner work together to identify individual learning needs and how these can be met.

It is difficult, however, to keep up to date with all the new ideas which are emerging in nursing today. Those working in educational staff support posts are in an ideal position to provide information about such ideas, as well as about identifying and preparing suitable learning experiences. The sorts of thing which may be included in this category are the use of nursing models, managing clinical changes and research in practice. The subjects are so wide-ranging that it is not always possible to provide local workshops, but there is a wealth of other choices available through such things as distance learning, the literature and local or national conferences.

One of the most successful approaches to staff development in recent times seems to be through the work of a facilitator – that is, someone who will work through a planned change with a group of clinical staff, providing information, teaching and, most importantly, support, but not directing people on what is 'good or bad'. The interest and support of a knowledgeable 'external change agent' can be a valuable asset in bringing about developments in practice.

Support Posts in Quality Assurance, Standards and Dependency

The use of dependency studies, that is, methods of trying to match nursing hours needed to nursing hours available, has been advocated for many years (e.g. Aberdeen, 1976; Telford, 1979). More recently, attention has been paid to quality assurance (Wandelt, 1974; Goldstone, 1983) and the establishment of standards for clinical practice (Kitson, 1986). These particular subjects were discussed in the previous chapter.

Besides the obvious benefits of these developments to patient care, they also serve as a very useful guide to clinical nurses by providing information about their current practice and identifying areas of excellence and those where there is room for development.

Indeed in some districts, the provision of a quality measurement service is only granted when requested by the senior clinical nurse of the unit, to whom the report is returned once completed. The rationale behind this is that the use of quality measures is indeed a service to clinical nurses, acting as a diagnostic tool in helping them to identify their strengths and weaknesses and, thus, areas where they may develop. There is always a risk that, if the service was 'imposed' by an external manager, it might be seen to be punitive in nature rather than as part of an accepted effort to develop professional practice.

Support Post – Services

One of the most time-consuming occupations which many senior clinical nurses have to fulfil is negotiating with other support services essential to the smooth running of the ward, such as catering, laundry and domestic services. In many instances, the most speedy answer to a problem seems to be to deal with it directly since it is often easier and quicker to do things oneself. So the trays are cleaned, the linen borrowed or the supplies fetched. Yet these are essentially non-nursing duties. While nobody minds dealing with such things from time to time in an emergency, continuing to do so is inappropriate and a poor use of nursing resources.

On the other side of the coin, suggestions or ideas connected with one of these support services and which could be of great value to the service overall often arise in clinical units; however, these are often passed by without being dealt with because of the time it would take to follow them through. It may be appropriate for a nurse in a staff support post to take the responsibility for acting upon such ideas and representing nurses in trying to solve these kinds of organisational problem. Again, it is obvious that co-operation is needed on all sides, with the provision of information by the clinical staff and a listening ear to the possible solutions.

Support Post – Equipment

How often have we found it difficult to make decisions about the wealth of different types of equipment which is now available for use in practice? Questions are always being asked about the cost in relation to the quality, and it is difficult to get accurate information on which to base decisions. The problems may appear to be very simple, such as a poor-quality paper towel leaving the hands wet and potentially chafed, or having to use a greater number of towels for the same job. Alternatively, they may be more technical in nature, such as discovering which is the most cost-effective and reliable suction equipment or pump.

It is this sort of information which is supplied to the public through consumer guides but which is less readily available for specialised equipment. Having someone working specifically in this area can be of great value to clinical staff, providing valuable information which would otherwise be difficult to obtain. It can also be a very cost-effective service in monetary terms. Causier (1982) describes how she developed the role of Equipment Nurse for one district, with very rewarding results from both the financial and the clinical viewpoints. She emphasises that it is not always cost-effective to use the cheapest equipment and that 'consumer involvement' is essential if the service is to work well.

Of course, someone working with these responsibilities cannot be effective without the help and support of those in clinical posts. In order to assess the effectiveness, as well as the cost, of different dressings or tapes, clinical trials have to take place with accurate assessment and evaluation. Similarly, if new equipment is to be tried and tested it has to be done in the environment in which it will be used. Alternatively, if there is a problem with equipment already in use, accurate information about the difficulty is needed if someone is to investigate the situation on the nurse's behalf.

Clinical Nurse Specialists

The staff support posts which have been described so far are those which, for the most part, are related to administrative or organisational issues. There are, however, also many nurse practitioners who have posts as clinical specialists with expertise in areas such as stoma care, diabetes or parenteral nutrition. Pearson (1983) describes a clinical nurse specialist as 'An expert practitioner of nursing with considerable skills and extensive experience in the care of patients in the speciality concerned'. Because their areas of interest are well defined they are in a good position to gain an understanding in depth of the particular speciality and, indeed, this is one of the reasons for the establishment of such posts. We cannot possibly be experts in all areas of nursing, especially as new knowledge is becoming available at such a fast rate, but one of the greatest skills of a generalist nurse is the ability to recognise what she does not know and to know where she can gain access to the services of experts who may give help or advice.

Clinical nurse specialists function in one of two ways; that is, by taking over one aspect of the care a client receives or by acting as a consultant with specialist knowledge about one aspect of care. In the first situation, they take over the responsibility for the whole cycle of care concerned with the specific problem, including the actual delivery of the service directly to patients. While at times this is very appropriate, it can also present some difficulties. Obviously, a specialist cannot be available for 24 hours a day, seven days a week, so timing has to be very carefully co-ordinated. Furthermore, unless a very effective communication network is established, it is easy to lose continuity of care for those components given by someone else.

Some people would argue that it is inappropriate actually to hand over one aspect of nursing to a clinical nurse specialist for two significant reasons, firstly, because of the problem of continuity but, secondly, because of the risk of the generalist becoming 'de-skilled' in that particular aspect of care. We all know that if we do not do something for a long period of time we can lose both our confidence and our technical skill; even though these can be regained quite quickly, they become rusty with lack of use. In the same way, if one aspect of care is always left for the specialist to 'do' then the skill of the general nurse may become rusty and real difficulties can arise when the specialist is away.

This leads to the second way in which clinical nurse specialists can work – as consultants and teachers. Rather than taking over the management of one aspect of patient care, their expertise is used in a consultative fashion, offering advice and information, and teaching both the patient and the nurse how to handle a particular situation. In this way their expertise is shared by many without the risk of lack of continuity or de-skilling. Very often there is a sigh of relief when a clinical nurse specialist is scheduled to visit a patient and a feeling that 'there will be one less thing to do today'. However, if clinical nurse specialists are to work as teachers and consultants, it does mean that it is essential that the nurse who works with the patient regularly (the primary nurse) is present when they visit. It is only through this means that she will be able to supply the continuity so essential for patient learning and good nursing.

It seems a shame that the work of specialists can so often be weakened by lack of continuity in their absence. The descriptions so far have applied solely to nurses working in specialist roles but exactly the same situations can arise with other experts. For example, a speech therapist can only visit a patient intermittently, yet many of the techniques and exercises which can help a patient to regain his or her lost speech lose their strength if they are not practised regularly. Help, encouragement and advice can only be offered by the nurse if she is also familiar with the regime which has been taught. Exactly the same principle can be applied to the work of the occupational therapist in teaching cooking skills: without the chance to practise, one session is of little value. The implications of all this are obvious, for the way in which one can work with others, rather than each person contributing his or her 'bit' in isolation, can lead to a much fuller service, and each person can strengthen the contribution of the other team members.

Some nurses have developed expertise in a particular aspect of nursing while still working as a senior clinical nurse in their unit or ward and they, too, can be called clinical nurse specialists. However, the way in whch they are consulted may vary because they are usually unable to leave their own units regularly. Nevertheless, they are in an excellent position to give advice over the telephone, to be visited or to give occasional seminars, lectures or guidelines. For instance, nurses working in hospices have gained great expertise in the management of pain in patients who are terminally ill, not just through the use of drugs but also with other methods. Their expertise and advice can be invaluable.

Many hospitals will have nurses filling other staff support posts, offering such things as counselling services, information technology and liaison. Some people take on more than one subject, becoming experts in more than one area; others will have a single function. However, it is important to remember that the way in which a service is used is just as important as how it is provided. Anyone who does not directly belong to the clinical team is essentially a visitor to the unit and, like visitors in one's own home or anywhere else, can be made to feel either welcome or unwanted. The reception they receive is essentially dependent on the behaviour of the 'hostess', in this instance the senior clinical nurse. The implication of this is that how those in staff support posts function depends as much on how they are used as on the way in which they work. Without being made to feel welcome their work cannot be effective. This returns to the issue that there is a responsibility on those using the service to make clear what they find helpful and then to give those providing the service welcome access.

Some units may be too small to provide a designated post of the kind described here. If this is the case, one solution may be to assign one of the qualified team members to be responsible for a particular aspect which would be useful to the unit as a whole. For example, one nurse may have worked locally for a long time and, over the years, have become very familiar with the workings of some of the other departments – it might be that if given the responsibility, she would be able to talk about catering services at a local level. This may not be the ideal way around the problem but at least the load would then be shared and should be easier to cope with.

Many units have not yet developed a system of staff support posts and continue with the traditional line management structure. Others have been influenced by the advent of the Griffiths management structure to reorganise their nursing structures, with the creation of such roles as quality assurance nurse at a senior level. It is not easy for those who have filled these new positions to shift from hierarchical ways of·working, where they have had authority over other nurses, to the provision of a service. Nor is it easy for clinical nurses to develop a collegial relationship with staff who have previously been line managers.

Learning has to take place on both sides if the services are to develop to their full potential. Yet the value of such an approach is infinite since it frees time for those who are actually delivering care to concentrate their efforts in that area and have access to facilities which will make that task easier. Even if such a facility is not available at the moment, surely it is worth striving for.

EXERCISE

1. Make a list of all the support services which are available to you in your district, including the services of paramedical colleagues who only visit your unit intermittently.

2. Describe those services you think would be useful in helping you to run your unit well.

3. Consider how you manage care in relationship to visits from experts from other specialities. Do you spend time with them or are they left to work alone? Could this be an agenda item for one of your ward meetings?

4. Do you or any members of your ward team have an expertise in a specific aspect of nursing? Is there a way in which that expertise could be shared with others?

Further Reading

Kinston W (1987) *Stronger Nursing Organisation*. London: Brunel Institute of Organisation and Social Structure.

14
Using Assertiveness Skills

This chapter aims to help you to:

- Be able to identify the differences between assertive, non-assertive and aggressive behaviours
- Appreciate the verbal and non-verbal components of assertive behaviour
- Be able to describe some ways of responding assertively in specific situations
  - giving and receiving praise
  - giving and receiving criticism
  - making requests

WHAT IS ASSERTIVE BEHAVIOUR?

People worry about what they say or do not say, whether they present themselves well or not and how much choice or control they have in the situations which confront them and to which they respond.

Since the 1960s, there has been an increasing interest in helping individuals to feel more in control of their lives, and this has partly focused on the need for people to develop an assertive approach to living. Courses and workshops aimed at developing the range of assertiveness techniques available to individuals have increased in number, as have the number of books and articles written on the subject; these all offer extremely practical methods for increasing the ability to function assertively.

Assertiveness is not an enduring personality trait which people do or do not possess, rather, it is an acquired adaptive social skill. Assertiveness techniques are not manipulative, but constructive tools to be used skillfully, as an effective means to an end. Galassi and Galassi (1981) have described assertive behaviour as:

'a type of interpersonal behaviour which allows an individual to act in her own best interests, without anxiety, to exercise her own rights without denying the rights of others.'

and

'. . . it is primarily a function of the situation and the interaction of the person and the situation.'

Assertive behaviour allows people to express their feelings and state their needs openly, and to exercise personal and professional rights, allowing those same rights to others. It increases the ability to handle positive or negative aspects of interactions and to achieve more positive outcomes.

Since it is situation-specific, people may behave assertively in one context, but choose not to in another (the emphasis is on the choice). The decision may be affected by a variety of factors such as the perceived status of the other person in the interaction, past experiences in similar situations, how much value is placed on the relationship, or the behaviour of the other person in the interaction. The consequences of non-assertive behaviour may also be taken into account.

Assertive people use methods of communicating which express their feelings, needs and opinions in an appropriate, honest, direct and focused way. They will negotiate, resolutely attempting neither to dominate others nor, at the other extreme, submit to others inappropriately.

Assertive behaviour does, however, involve risks. Assertive people may not always get what they want or if they do they may not gain the approval of others and this in itself can lead to internal conflicts. However, at least they will have tried and will not, if they have won, feel that in trying they have violated the rights of others.

WHY DO NURSES NEED TO BEHAVE ASSERTIVELY?

With the emphasis on individualised, holistic care, the need for assisting patient advocacy and ensuring high standards of care has become even more apparent. Indeed, it forms part of the 'UKCC Code of Professional Practice' (UKCC, 1984):

> Item 1: 'Act always in such a way as to promote and safeguard the well-being and interests of patients/clients.'

> Item 2: 'Have regard to the environment of care and its physical, psychological and social effects on patients/clients and also to the adequacy of resources, and make known to the appropriate person or authorities any circumstances which could place patients/clients in jeopardy or which militate against safe standards of practice.'

Legally and ethically, qualified nurses are responsible for their actions, yet often do not have the authority or power to make decisions which fall within their sphere of work. For instance, if staffing levels in a unit are falling below a level which the nurse in charge feels is safe it may only be the senior manager who can decide to call in agency staff, or increase the establishment. Decisions of this nature are fraught with difficulty which is made worse by the conflict which can occur between professional and organisational responsibilities.

Traditionally, nursing has nurtured non-assertive, passive behaviour. In a largely female profession the cultural norms of 'female submissive role' and 'female professional role' under the dominance of male administrators and doctors have been praised, valued and encouraged. In the past, nurses were trained to be quiet, obedient followers, unquestioning in their interactions with other professionals. With the developing professional role we need nurses who are confident in their knowledge and ability to act as a support to patients and, if necessary, act as their advocates. Similarly, we need those who are independent decision-makers, able to tackle areas of work where different opinions exist, and where there is potential for disagreement. Donnelly (1978) has said: 'Assertive nurses can change the whole health care system'. Whether you believe this or not, behaving assertively will at least help you to feel more in control of your professional practice.

There is also a need for each nurse to be a self-advocate. We all have needs to be met and rights to respect, privacy, personal space and time outside our professional lives. With increased patient throughput, diminishing resources and reduced staffing levels these factors are often forgotten. Could this be you . . . ?

> Taking on extra shifts or working late when the ward is short-staffed; being available to listen to everyone else's troubles whilst having plenty of your own; coping with each new crisis that arrives despite feeling resentment and exhaustion; feeling that you've got to keep going, no matter what because you're the senior person on duty and if you crack whatever will the rest do! Knowing you've become the person who will always say 'yes' and hating it, but worried that saying 'no' will lead to conflict . . .

If this is you, isn't it time that you looked at the situation objectively and asked why? An understanding of the beliefs and behaviours inherent in being assertive may help. You may have to change your current behaviour, though, and change threatens the equilibrium, causes some disruption and can therefore be an anxiety-provoking exercise. If this is not for you, read no further. However, being able to cope with change is another important aspect of learning to be more assertive.

DIFFERENTIATING ASSERTIVE BEHAVIOUR

There are, essentially, four ways in which people act in any 'difficult' situation. Together they form a continuum as shown in Figure 14.1.

On the whole, people rely on one style of behaviour more than another, even though they may not be totally consistent. There are positive and negative effects with each of these modes of response. Note, though, that the following pen pictures tend to be rather stereotyped images and, as such, exaggerate the differences in order to highlight them. It is also worth pointing out that there are times when one may intentionally choose not to be assertive without having to behave in any of the ways described below; these only become apparent when used as a regular response.

The Submissive Approach

The submissive approach is self-denying. People who behave in this way lack respect for their own feelings, needs and concerns. They seldom express their rights, or do so in such an indirect or diffident manner that no-one takes them seriously. They constantly allow others to make decisions for them. They communicate to others that their feelings, needs and opinions do not matter as much as those of others. They are often terse, fidgety, whining, hesitant people whose whole demeanour, from a lack of eye contact and a hunched posture to a timid facial expression, shows their defeated stance.

The benefits of this sort of behaviour include the possible approval of others, especially aggressive types, since they are seen as selfless, nice people who say and do nothing to affect or hinder

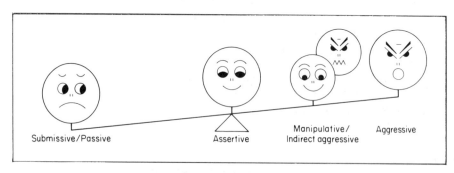

Fig 14.1 A continuum of responses

others. Conflict is postponed or avoided by 'giving in'. This response can, however, also be used to manipulate, especially if other people feel guilty that yet again they have 'got their way'.

The price, however, lies in the cost of allowing others constantly to violate their perceived rights. The resentment generated can be repressed or denied only for so long – some day it will find expression, perhaps as an aggressive outburst triggered by a seemingly trivial happening and vented on an innocent party, or through actual physical illness.

The Aggressive Approach

The aggressive approach is both self-enhancing and attacking. Those who behave in this way infer that other people matter less than they do. They express their opinions, feelings and needs at the expense of others, so infringing on their rights. Implicit in any interaction is the fact that they intend to win, whatever the cost. Aggressive people overpower and dominate subordinates. They tower over people, standing very close, invading personal space. They speak loudly and have accompanying attacking body movements such as pointing with the finger, hand-waving and frowning. They often make direct verbal attacks on the person, rather than on the behaviour exhibited, making sarcastic, disrespectful or rude comments, blaming the other person and 'putting them down'. They insist on having the last word on matters which they feel are important.

The benefit of this kind of behaviour is, of course, that they usually get what they want by browbeating everyone else into submission. The price, however, is that they are generally unlikeable people and, therefore, lonely and prone to feelings of vulnerability and, if they are not completely impervious to the feelings of others, often of guilt. There is also always the chance that, at some time, someone will fight back equally aggressively.

The Manipulative Approach

The manipulative approach is subtle, covert, aggressive behaviour. People who use this devious approach have their needs met by means of making others feel guilty if they do not comply with requests. They make decisions affecting themselves and others while giving the impression that others have actually made their own decisions. Their verbal and non-verbal messages often conflict. They say something rather nasty in a sweet tone of voice and with a smile on their face. Their gestures are often very friendly, they get almost too close for comfort when talking, but avoid eye contact at crucial moments.

The benefit is that they can 'fool some of the people some of the time', and therefore find their needs met, but the price is that they can't 'fool everybody all of the time'. Sooner or later they will not have their own way.

The Assertive Approach

The assertive approach means knowing exactly what is wanted but not trampling on others to achieve it. Assertive people cope with situations appropriately asking openly and directly for needs to be met, but are not demoralised if these needs are not met on every occasion. They will ask in a relaxed calm manner, making appropriate eye contact and body movements, and will listen attentively to the response. They preserve good relationships through successful negotiation. They acknowledge their strengths and weaknesses, and accept responsibility for the choices they make.

The benefits are that they feel at ease with themselves and, because of this, others feel at ease with them. Assertiveness reduces tension and anxiety and helps all concerned to know where they stand. Each is aware of his or her own rights and feels comfortable in expressing them but will afford others the same respect. Dickson (1982) and Smith (1975) have both discussed rights and the following list is adapted from their views.

Assertive Rights

- I have the right to state my own needs and set my own priorities as a person, independently of others or of roles I assume.
- I have the right to ask for what I want.
- I have the right to be treated with respect as an intelligent, capable and equal human being.
- I have the right to express my feelings, opinions and values.
- I have the right to judge my own behaviour and take responsibility for the consequences of that behaviour.
- I have the right to say, 'No' or 'Yes' for myself.
- I have the right to change my mind.
- I have the right to say I don't understand and ask for more information.
- I have the right to make mistakes and to take responsibility for those mistakes.

- I have the right to interact with others without being dependent upon them for approval.

We need to be aware of these rights both as people and as nurses. We must examine our own belief systems; if we accept that we have these rights as people and nurses do we also believe that these same rights extend to others? A belief in a 'right' can be helpful in increasing assertive behaviour.

BECOMING MORE ASSERTIVE

Remember you always have a choice. You can be submissive, manipulative, aggressive or assertive but, if you choose assertive behaviour, the chances of getting what you want are increased. The assertive response is judged to be socially competent and effective, and equally potent to, and more desirable than, aggressive behaviour. There is a catch! It is seen as distinctly less likeable than submissive behaviour! Nevertheless, many feel that the advantages far outweigh the disadvantages.

The development of self-awareness and a sense of self-worth are essential prerequisites to assertive behaviour. It also involves developing awareness of the way verbal messages are received. In an assertive response these are congruent, so that the message is clear and direct and the recipient is not left feeling concerned or confused.

Verbal Ways of Improving Assertiveness

1. *Use 'I' statements*   Assume responsibility for your own feelings and behaviour.

For instance: 'I lose my patience and get angry when you are late'

rather than: 'You make me lose patience and get angry when . . .'

2. *Change verbs*   Change 'can't to 'won't' where appropriate and 'have to' to 'choose to'.

For instance: 'I choose to visit my elderly aunt tonight even though I feel tired because she gets lonely'

rather than: 'I have to visit my elderly aunt . . .'

Changing 'need' to 'want' encourages realistic appraisal of the difference.

3. *Be specific*   Decide what it is you want or feel beforehand and then say so, honestly and directly. Make a clear, succinct statement.

Avoid unnecessary waffle, flannel or apologies, so that the focus of concern is not obscured and the impact lost; such as, 'I'm terribly sorry, and I know you said you might have something on but I'd like you to change your off duty next Saturday'. You may wish to add a reason, of course, but do not pad your statement.

If you are not immediately successful persist and try . . .

4. *Repetition – the 'broken record'* Repeat your statement calmly and steadily, perhaps rephrasing it slightly. Deflect any attempts to undermine or sidetrack your assertive response. Listen to the reply and repeat the statement again, if necessary. However, do be prepared to negotiate when appropriate.

5. *Field the response – 'fogging'* Show that you have heard a response by repeating or paraphrasing it. Respond to the relevant comments and answer any questions that have been asked.

For instance: 'I understand when you say you'd like to keep Saturday free in case you're asked to a party, but I'd still like you to change your off-duty. Is there a way we can get round this one?'

6. *Self-disclosure* In a difficult situation, disclose your feelings with a simple statement such as, 'I feel nervous' or, 'I feel guilty'. Getting feelings into the open can help you to relax and begin to take charge of yourself.

7. *Voice and speech pattern* An assertive voice is steady, medium-volume, and warm. Before any difficult situation, consciously breath slowly and deeply. This helps to reduce tension in the throat and produces a more relaxed, audible voice.

Non-Verbal Ways of Improving Assertiveness

Become aware of your body – it expresses what you are feeling in both positive and negative ways. If you are feeling assertive then this is likely to be reflected in your non-verbal behaviours. Becoming aware of the language of your body means that you can learn to keep its expression under control. For instance, judgments of assertiveness are strongly influenced by the overall facial expression (Romano and Bellack, 1980).

Facial expression should be appropriate and calm. Smile when pleased (not a fixed grin); frown when displeased (but not a scowl).

Eye contact: the gaze should be relaxed and direct without staring. Remember that the eyes have been described as the mirror of the soul.

The mouth and jaw should be relaxed. Do not clench your jaw or purse your lips. If there is an opportunity before a difficult situation, exercise your facial muscles: move your jaw about, open and close your mouth widely, while breathing deeply and evenly.

Gestures should be used only to emphasise points and should be slow and steady with open hand movements, not clenched fists.

Body movements: stand or sit upright and relaxed. Do not fidget from foot to foot or wriggle in a chair. Watch for your hands fiddling with hair, jewellery or clothing. Do not cover your mouth or constantly chew your lip.

Proximity – do not encroach unduly on the other person's personal space. Try to get on the same level as the other person, not tower over them.

While the examples given above are all recommended ways of becoming more assertive they must be taken as general guides rather than essential activities. Some people find them helpful while others will discover more appropriate ways for themselves and it is up to the individual to find a way which suits him or her personally.

Assertiveness in Difficult Situations

Asking for What You Want

Remember you have the 'right' to ask for what you want and your best chance of getting it is *to work out exactly what it is you want*. Work out how, when and where you will make the request – Phelps and Austin (1975) call this the principle of action rather than reaction; making the first move can make you feel more in control than waiting around for someone else to take the initiative. Put the request clearly and concisely, making sure you have the other person's undivided attention. If you do not get the response you wish and it is important to you, repeat the request, equally clearly, with an explanation of why it is important.

Refusing Requests and Saying No

There can be positive effects to saying 'no' when you mean it. It reduces the resentment you might feel if you said 'yes' unwillingly. It means that you will not feel exploited by neglecting your own needs at the expense of helping others, and you will not feel guilty when you make excuses later not to meet the request.

Think about what happens when a request is made.

- Your immediate 'gut response' could be a better guide than your head; it may tell you what you really want to say. How often have you said later, 'I wish I'd said what I really felt'.
- If 'oughts' or 'shoulds' come to mind, ask for more information about the commitment that a 'yes' would bring.
- Try, 'I need time to think about it', and negotiate when you will respond (remember very few requests need an instantaneous decision).
- If your response is 'no', make both verbal and non-verbal components of the message clear and direct. Give a reason if you wish, apologise if you must, but do not become submissive or defensive. If your 'no' is clear you may be pleasantly surprised to find that it is accepted.
- However if it is not, 'field the response' restating your 'no'.
- Accept your feelings of anxiety if this is the first occasion on which you have asserted your 'right' to say no. It may cause a bit of consternation on this first time because it is unexpected: it gets easier with practice!
- If it is appropriate, tell the person how you feel on rejecting the request. Remember that you are rejecting this request on this occasion, not the person.
- Once you have refused the request, end the discussion of that topic, otherwise the person might think you want to be persuaded to change your mind. However, rather than walking away try to introduce a new topic of conversation as a means of showing that there are no 'hard feelings'.
- Lastly, but importantly, remember you have the 'right' to change your mind if you persist in feeling guilty.

Praise

We all need feedback on our performance – both positive and negative. In most work situations we find that we hear about our mistakes rapidly but, particularly in nursing, we have to assume that if we are not criticised then all must be well. A dearth of positive feedback can actually have a negative effect on performance: praise motivates, and improves interpersonal relationships. We like to hear that we are doing well, or have special skills or attributes that are valued. It is a good reward, and can help to build self-confidence and thus improve performance.

Giving Praise

Initially, we may need to overcome the embarrassment that expressing our good feelings about another person may produce. Be specific – do not just say 'well done' and rush away. Give a clear description of the specific behaviour you are recognising and valuing; for instance, 'You coped really well with that dressing and it wasn't the easiest to do. Mrs X (patient) says she would like you to do it for her again tomorrow, which is praise indeed!'

Accepting a Compliment

Usually we tend to deny praise – 'It wasn't that difficult really.' This puts the other person down. You are correcting a judgment she has made, in other words telling her that she is mistaken. The other thing we do is become suspicious: 'What does she want now?'

If the verbal and non-verbal components of the message feel right then acknowledge that you have heard the remark so that the person knows it has not been dismissed or rejected. Acknowledgement does not mean that you agree – but think about it, you might feel better about yourself!

Criticism

Criticism can be valuable if it is constructive and valid. It may enable a person to recognise and deal with a problem. We have the right to honest information about our performance, and we have the responsibility to be open enough to hear it even if we do not like it.

Criticism can be:

- *Valid* The comments made are accurate or true
- *Invalid* The comments are untrue, and may be being used to hurt or humilitate. Assertive people do not use invalid criticism. However, some people may genuinely see a situation differently, so bear this in mind and remember that there can be acceptable differences of opinion.
- *Partly valid* There may be some truth in the statement in general, but in this instance the facts are overstated; assertive people clarify the facts and change it into valid criticism. It is also worth remembering that just because you are assertive you may not always be right!

Giving Criticism

- Remember that you have the 'right' to ask for what you want. This may be for a change in someone's behaviour. If you do not ask, the resentment that builds up will affect your relationship with that person.
- Take the initiative (action *v* reaction principle); choose the time and place to make the problem plain; acknowledge the good points in that person and then describe the behaviour you find difficult, stating, if appropriate, how this behaviour affects you. Specify the change you expect: 'I'm pleased with the effort you put into your work when you are on duty; however, I feel angry and put-upon when you arrive late as you have done five times in the last two weeks. Is there some reason behind this that we can do something about, because I would like you to start punctually in the future?'
- Explain the positive effects if your request is met, and the possible negative outcome if it is ignored, such as, 'I would feel much more supported if you were on duty at the start of the shift', or, 'I will have to take formal action if your lateness continues'.
- Let the recipient give any information they wish but do not be sidetracked or manipulated.
- Encourage people to find their own solutions to problems, but let them know that you are available if they need help.
- Share your feelings about giving the criticism, if appropriate, then let it go and allow the people time to improve.

Receiving Criticism

If criticism is unexpected it can be extremely hurtful, but if we know it is coming then we feel tense, anxious and defensive.

- Listen to what the person has to say.
- Take time to think whether it is valid, partly valid or invalid criticism, and then respond steadily and calmly.
- If the criticism is valid, accept it – remember that you have the 'right' to make mistakes. Acknowledging the criticism also often helps to reduce anxiety and defensiveness.
- You may wish to give a reason for your behaviour or ask for more information to clarify the problem for you.
- Say what you will try to do to rectify the matter.
- Offer a positive statement about yourself if possible.

- If the criticism is invalid, disagree calmly and assertively, making your response with conviction, 'No, I'm not always late and I don't like your making that statement. I was late yesterday because my car wouldn't start, but this was the first time in months.' This is usually effective but if it is not then try 'wearing the person down: '. . . What do you mean, I'm always late?' continuing, 'Well, if you're now saying I was late once last week why did you say I'm always late?', and so on. If the criticism is invalid, the other person will eventually wish that she had never raised the matter in the first place!

'Crumple Buttons'

This is the description used by Anne Dickson (1982) for those particular chinks that we have in our defensive armour which, whenever touched, produce strong emotions for us. It may be a word, 'You're bossy/lazy/scruffy'; it may be an area of comment, perhaps animal rights or academic nurses, or a particular tone of voice that someone uses. Whatever it is we know we fall apart when this 'crumple button' is touched. We each need to identify our own 'crumple button' and to recognise our immediate responses when it is pushed in order to begin to take control of our emotions.

With all this examination of your verbal and non-verbal inter-actions, and thinking before you act, you may feel that becoming more assertive is tedious and laborious and not at all you. Do not worry, it will develop with practice into a skill which is very much a part of your whole response to life.

Practice the techniques first in situations which are not highly emotionally charged and with people who do not know you well, such as shop assistants who chatter about what they did last night when you wish to be served, or the person who pushes in front of you in the queue. Remember also that there is no one model of assertiveness. Situations are unique, and our responses must be flexible enough to allow for modification or to be adjusted to the particular context and content of the interaction.

Try to avoid an instant major change to your preferred behaviour; this may be too much for you, and particularly others! Adopt a style which feels appropriate for you personally, bearing in mind that behaving assertively and consistently may ensure that more of your needs are met than would be by being inconsistently submissive or aggressive. It may help you to feel just a little bit more in control of both your personal and your professional life.

1. Write down five things you like about yourself. (Do not qualify the items with 'sometimes' or 'quite', or words such as these.)

2. In the following situations, think of how:

(i) you would normally respond
(ii) you could respond assertively.

- A colleague asks to borrow one of your textbooks; she is well known for not returning items she borrows.
- You ask a doctor to see some relatives who are very worried about their father. He says he is too busy.
- You overhear a student nurse on the bus discussing a patient by name.
- A friend asks you to a party which you really do not want to go to.

3. Take the plunge! Discuss the problem with that person at work which you have been putting off until now.

Further Reading

Bolton R (1986) *People Skills.* Brookvale, NSW: Prentice Hall.

Cox G and Dianow F (1986) *Making the Most of Yourself.* London:

Sheldon Press.

Dickson A (1982) *A Woman in Her Own Right. Assertiveness and You.* London: Quartet Books.

15
Introducing Change

This chapter aims to introduce you to:

- The way in which people commonly respond to change
- Some principles which apply to change
- The change process
- A way in which change can be planned

According to Lippitt (1973), change is 'any planned or unplanned alteration in status quo of an organism, situation, or process'. In the introductory chapters, recent alterations in the status quo and the implications for nursing work were identified. It is the purpose here to examine:

- Reaction to change
- The method or activities involved in achieving an alteration in status quo
- The role of the agent of change

REACTION TO CHANGE

People respond or react to change in different ways. Two aspects of human reaction are identified here for consideration, namely resistance, in relation to the nature and magnitude of the change itself, and the emotional cycle which is commonly experienced during the change process. These aspects are raised for discussion since an understanding of why they occur and an insight into the way in which they are manifested will have considerable influence on the chance of achieving a successful outcome in any change venture.

Resistance to Change

It would appear that, in general, people are creatures of habit and will protect the familiar by resisting change. However, it is also recognised by most of us, that change is a part of our everyday lives and must, therefore, be considered as inevitable. Is it then, a quirk of human nature which causes us to resist that which is known to be inevitable? Many years ago, Machiavelli (c. 1513) when writing of change made the following comments:

'It must be considered that there is nothing more difficult . . . doubtful of success . . . dangerous to handle, than to initiate a new order of things. For the reformer has enemies in all those who profit by the old order and only lukewarm defenders in all those who profit by the new order . . . partly because of the incredulity of mankind, who do not truly believe in anything new until they have had actual experience of it.'

In the light of these comments, made more than four centuries ago, it can be seen that human nature does not alter and resistance must be considered to be a fundamental component of the change process. An understanding of why people resist and ways in which resistance is manifested can go some way towards helping to smooth the path of change, and is therefore an important prerequisite to planning.

Resistance is commonly viewed in two ways: resistance which effectively hampers and blocks change, and resistance which maintains order and stability. Resistance can be considered to be both good and bad: bad in terms of preventing or blocking something which may be advantageous or even essential; good in terms of tempering and balancing, thus preventing a headlong dash into a situation without prior planning.

The degree of resistance shown depends upon several factors, including:

- Feelings of inadequacy and lack of power to bring about the change
- How radical the change is and how different things will be from the current situations, particularly in relationship to value systems and beliefs
- How much participants value and hold dear the old days
- How advantageous the change will be to the participants
- How much it will cost (money)
- How much inconvenience it will cause
- Worries on the part of the participating individuals in terms of role, status, power, freedom, responsibilities, accountability and the need to learn new skills
- Perceptions of the change agent in terms of role and credibility

It cannot be denied that resistance is inherent in the change process and the factors identified above influence the degree to which it may occur. There are, however, several classic ways in which resistance is manifested, and it is worth noting them since a watch can then be kept for their presence. The sorts of behaviour which may occur include:

1. *Lip service*   In this case, people will listen to suggestions and even contribute ideas when the person initiating the change is present, but when it comes to action they are no longer prepared to do anything: they may be helpful when the change agent is present but certainly not in his or her absence.

2. *Aggression*   It is not unusual for people to manifest aggressive behaviour when they are unhappy about change. In many ways this can be seen as a protective mechanism in an attempt not to have to face the presenting situation.

3. *Destruction*   Destructive behaviour may also occur from time to time. People will actually try to put a stop to the change, possibly because the effects may be threatening or unacceptable to them. Sometimes destructive behaviour can be open but at other times it may be manifested in more obscure ways; for example, sympathising, rather than empathising with those who are going through change can reinforce a feeling of self-pity and destroy people's commitment to the planned change. Yet this is a very common type of behaviour which has to be guarded against.

4. *Lack of Continuity*   How often have we made excuses for not trying new methods on one occasion. All sorts of excuses are put up: 'We're too busy today so we won't bother' or, 'There are too many new staff'. Gradually, the excuses become weaker and weaker: 'It's Sunday so we'll give ourselves a day off' or, 'It's Jane's birthday so we'll have a treat'. Slowly and surely this type of behaviour will undermine a change and after a period of time it will die a natural death, hidden in some dusty recess of our minds.

It is essential, then, to minimise resistance, so allowing change to happen but in a balanced, controlled manner. Some of the ways in which resistance can be minimised are:

- Clarification of outcome – people need to know what they are working towards
- Matching of resources needed and resources available including money, manpower, tools and equipment and educational programmes
- Clarification of implications for all participants
- Effective communication between all parties
- Effective handling of problems as they arise

- Careful planning
- Careful selection of change agents
- Credibility of the change agent

One of the most effective ways of minimising resistance is actively to involve people at all stages of the process. Giving people the opportunity to contribute and become part of the change personally involves them and offers them the chance to help rather than hinder. It can create a feeling of worth and recognition. It is often worth while compromising on some aspects in order to achieve those things which are seen to be essential.

Another strategy which has been found to be helpful in minimising resistance is to negotiate an agreed trial period. If people feel that they will not have to go on for ever, they are sometimes willing to try something new. So the suggestion that a new way of organising work or a new approach to assessment will only be tried for six or eight weeks, with the promise of a review at the end of that time, can often get things off the ground. If this strategy is used, however, it is essential that the promise of a review is upheld.

EMOTIONAL REACTIONS

The second predictable response to change is concerned with emotional reactions. The emotional cycle of change, described by Kelley and Conner (1979), relates to the feelings experienced by people participating in change. Emotions of the participants fluctuate from highs to lows and it would appear that these 'highs' and 'lows' can be identified with particular stages in the change process.

Things usually start off with a 'high', before the participants become fully aware of what they are really letting themselves in for. This stage is referred to as *uninformed optimism*. The stage of *informed pessimism* begins when people begin to recognise the full implications of the change and, perhaps, come up against problems. This is the point at which some participants may even wish to withdraw so plans need to be laid to help them through. However, with acknowledgement, support and perhaps some restructuring, hope will begin to be generated, the stage of *hopeful realism*. Hope, and some evidence of a return for the efforts which have been made, instils confidence in the venture and is known as the stage of *informed optimism*. This sees the participants through to *rewarding completion* which brings the glow of satisfaction (Figure 15.1).

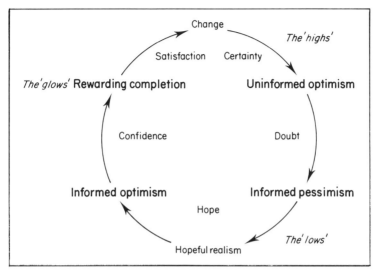

Fig 15.1   The emotional response to change

THE METHOD OR ACTIVITIES OF CHANGE

If a desired alteration in the status quo is to be achieved, planned and purposeful activity is necessary. This is in contrast to unplanned and undirected activity where the outcome is largely dependent upon chance. Planned change is 'an intended, designed, or purposeful attempt by an individual, group, organisation, or larger social system to influence the status quo of itself, another organisation, or a situation' (Lippitt, 1973).

When planning change there are always two major areas for consideration, namely the individuals concerned and the organisation within which the change will occur. If either is ignored then the chances of smooth progress are lessened. Schein (1969) suggests that individuals 'seek to live in a state of equilibrium'. If something happens to disrupt that equilibrium, such as the acquisition of new knowledge, an uncomfortable state of dissonance can occur where what we know does not match the way we behave.

Two courses of action can be taken. Firstly, the new knowledge can be denied, devalued or ignored. Alternatively, there must be a change in behaviour to take into account what has recently been learnt. Exactly the same principle applies in our everyday lives with such things as the use of a new piece of equipment. If time is not taken to learn how it works and to practise handling it then it can easily be rejected as useless, hidden at the back of a cupboard and ignored. New knowledge can be treated in the same way.

According to Lewin (1951) organisations 'work as a result of a dynamic balance of forces working in opposite directions with equal pull'. Many organisations are made up of a number of subsections, which interface, one with another. For instance, within the health service there are subsections concerned with catering, supplies, medicine and many other things, all of which, at some time or another, need to interact with nursing. Over a period of time they have found a balance and, with a bit of give and take, have learnt to live together with compromises made on both sides. For example, as nurses in an ideal world, it would be desirable to have a 24-hour catering service with a wide range of foods available at any time of the day and night. As far as the catering service is concerned, ideally they may like to have a steady demand made on their services at the same time each day, serving people with the same tastes and appetites. Obviously, neither of these is possible but compromises have been made on both sides so that some choice of menu is offered but, on the whole, meals are served within an agreed range of times.

However, suppose that a microwave oven became available to the unit, as is happening in many places; the flexibility which this offers in terms of timing of meals could potentially disrupt the relationship between nursing and catering. Unless both parties are involved at the planning stages when such a change occurs then the relationship between the two subsections can be disturbed. Thus, recognition of the effect which a change in nursing will have on other parts of the organisation and the early involvement of all parties concerned can save many headaches at a later stage.

As discussed in Chapter 2, the action research model may be applied to any organised procedure. If a desired change is brought about by a planned procedure, it is appropriate to describe the method or activities of change in the same way. The method or activity of change may then be referred to as the 'change process', and this process involves the same seven discrete activities which are discussed below.

Activity 1: Data Collection

When responding to a proposed change, two distinct sets of data are required. The first set will describe the current situation. The second set will describe both the desired outcome which it is hoped will be achieved following implementation of the change and the resources required. It is absolutely crucial that these two sets of data should be compared to determine whether the proposed change is either necessary or practicable.

The following are examples of the types of data which might need to be collected; this is by no means an exhaustive list, the actual data required being dependent on each individual situation.

- Values and beliefs relating to people, their environment and health
- Pertinent knowledge, skills, attitudes and personality traits of all those involved in the change. This may not be restricted to nurses if others are involved
- Information about the environment and organisational constraints which may affect the planned change
- Personal characteristics and dependency of the client group, which will include health status
- The method of nursing used
- The structure and organisation of nursing work
- The budget which is available
- Communication networks
- Staffing levels and qualifications, both statutory and specialist
- Duty rosters
- Local policy and procedures
- Legislation
- Professional guidelines
- Work of other disciplines
- Sources of organisation power

The list is endless but, as can be seen, there is a very wide variety of data which could be pertinent to introducing different types of change. Some of it is easy to gather, for example, the way in which nursing work is organised, but other areas are more sensitive such as people's views and feelings on particular subjects. It is sometimes wise to start work on less sensitive issues initially until people's confidence is built up.

Activity 2: Analysis of Data

As already stated, careful analysis and comparison of data, referring to both current and desired situations, is required. This will enable decisions to be made about:

- Whether the proposed change is actually necessary and/or desirable
- Whether the proposed change is achievable in practice

It also offers a base against which progress can be measured in the future. Unless accurate information is gathered about the starting point, it is difficult to judge what progress has been made, and those involved can become disheartened. This is especially important at the stage of 'informed pessimism', described above and, unless there is a reminder available of how much progress has been made, people can run out of energy and give up.

Activity 3: Setting Objectives or Goals

Having established that the proposed change is both desirable and achievable, objectives need to be determined. Objectives are simply detailed statements of the desired outcome to be achieved and will include time-limits. Again, their determination is an essential activity, since no judgment can be made about the degree of progress unless a statement has been made about what the work is intended to achieve.

At this point it is worth clarifying for the purpose of this discussion the relationship between aims and objectives. An *aim* is considered to be the overall summary statement of the desired outcome and is generally complex and multifactorial. The *objectives* relate to the identifiable, individual factors encompassed within the aim. In this context, the change to a personalised service can be considered an aim. However, the concept of a personalised service is many-faceted and is influenced by many different things. These factors have to be identified individually and objectives or goals set for each one.

Activity 4: Identification of Possible Action Pathways

Firstly, this activity involves the identification of all possible avenues or pathways which may lead to the desired objective(s) and, secondly, each pathway is then explored to reveal the components and the ordered progression of action.

Activity 5: Selection of an Action Pathway

There is usually more than one way to achieve a desired objective, so careful analysis of all possible options is required. This analysis is influenced by a number of factors, for example:

- Knowledge derived from research
- The law
- Morality and ethics

- The chosen framework of practice
- Available technology
- Analysis of the relevant data (activities 1 and 2)
- Economics
- Common sense
- Professional judgment
- Intuition
- Local policy

When choosing a way forward, some people decide to tackle all components of a situation at one go. It may be decided that the parts of the whole process are so closely interlinked that they must all be moved through together in order to achieve the overall aim. For example, if the change is concerned with making care more personalised, it may be agreed to look at the method of work organisation, planning care, documentation, approaches to assessment and evaluation simultaneously. If this path is chosen it will obviously require extensive planning and energy beforehand.

Others may choose to break an aim into smaller parts and tackle each one separately: for example, assessment could be handled first before work is undertaken to improve evaluation. In this way, a complete cycle can be achieved in a shorter length of time and the pleasure of 'rewarding completion' experienced.

It sometimes happens that, once people have begun to change their practice, they become keen to tackle the whole project and, on occasion, this may be appropriate. However, it should be remembered that change does take extra energy and, if you already work in a very busy environment, it is often better to move slowly and carefully. The extra demands which are placed on people throughout the change process may be too much and this is often the cause of their giving up, especially at the danger point of 'informed pessimism'. If this is allowed to happen, all the previous efforts and goodwill can be lost, and it is twice as difficult to persuade people to start a second time as they will remember the unpleasant experience of failure in the first round. So as a word of warning, it is often better to do one small thing well than to try to change the world.

Activity 6: Implementation of an Action Pathway

The actual means of implementation will be dictated by the pathway which has been selected. However, it is essential during implementation that deliberate observations are made as these allow the success, or otherwise, of the action to be evaluated critically in relation to the unique setting in which it has been used.

It is also important at this stage to keep a careful eye on the whole procedure and watch for any signs of resistance. If people are finding the change too difficult they sometimes start to demonstrate some of the signs of stress such as increased sickness, moodiness or withdrawal (see Chapter 10) and these need to be picked up quickly in order that they can be handled.

Holding regular meetings, even if these are very short, in order to discuss progress is one way of reducing this effect. Involvement of all those concerned, recognition of their contribution and assurance that they are fully informed of progress all help to avoid this happening.

Activity 7: Analysis and Evaluation

Observations are analysed for effect in both qualitative and quantitative terms. The effect or actual outcome is then compared with the desired outcomes or objectives in order to establish the success, or otherwise, of the change process. If the early stages have been rushed or omitted, it is impossible to know at the end of the day whether or not it has been successful and the chance of reward, in terms of a feeling of achievement, is lost. Without this feeling it is much more difficult to tackle the next change endeavour.

THE ROLE OF THE NURSE PRACTITIONER AS THE AGENT OF CHANGE

Having identified the elements of the change process, the question must now arise as to who can act as a change agent and be responsible and accountable for the venture. In order to answer this question, it is helpful to undertake an analysis of the process to reveal the activities for which the change agent will be both responsible and accountable. From these activities, the necessary qualities for a successful agent of change can be identified:

- Identification of all parties to be involved in the change, including the power-holders in the hierarchy and other related services
- Establishment of a credible relationship with those to be involved in the change
- Collection of data within set time-limits, either personally or by delegation (bearing in mind that involvement is one way of reducing resistance!)

- Communication of objectives and time-limits to everyone involved
- Consideration of any worries which others may express and demonstration that they have been heard and, where possible, adjustments have been made
- Preparation of the timetable or work schedule for each step
- Establishment of the control points, such as regular feedback sessions
- Determination of where and when progress will be reviewed in relation to the objectives and implementation of any adjustments that might be necessary
- Clarification of responsibilities and lines of accountability for those carrying out delegated actions
- Encouragement of active participation by everyone involved
- Awarding of credit where due, and recognition of individual and collective effort
- Maintenance of records

At first sight, this list may look overwhelming but in fact the activities identified are no more than those of any good manager and which many people exercise on a day-to-day basis, anyway. However, in order to undertake these activities, it can be seen that those fulfilling the role of change agent do require some special skills, abilities and personal qualities:

- Organisation
- Planning
- Consultation
- Communication

- Persuasion
- Credibility
- Self-awareness

It is worth while to note here that a change agent may not be, and does not necessarily have to be, the most powerful person in terms of the nursing hierarchy. However, if the desired outcomes are to be achieved it is essential that the support of the 'power source' is obtained through regular communication and persuasion in respect to the value of the change.

In brief, then, the change agent generates ideas, introduces innovation, develops a climate for planned change by overcoming resistance and understanding forces for acceptance, and implements and evaluates the change (Lancaster J, in Lancaster and Lancaster, 1982). Bennis (1970) describes the change agent as being more than a man of action – he must be a professional who draws on a body of scientific knowledge.

In the light of the discussion in Chapter 13 relating to the development of support posts, it may be suggested that it would be appropriate to consider the creation of a clinical nurse/support post with the identified responsibilities of a change agent. The post holder may be appointed from either inside or outside the area where change is desired and there are advantages and disadvantages associated with both inside and outside appointments. The outsider does not have such a great degree of familiarity with the situation but, on the other hand, she comes to the situation with uncluttered vision and has nothing to gain personally. The insider knows the situation and people well and is familiar with their ways, but could be seen to be influenced by vested interests and be biased when making judgments. Change agents, then, are selected on the basis of matching their qualities with the change situations in which they will be involved.

Understanding of the role is one of the major factors which influences the effectiveness of a change agent. This understanding is necessary both by the change agent and by the participants in the change venture if conflict and tension are to be minimised.

EXERCISES

1. Identify a *simple, small* situation which you would like to change (e.g. keeping a notice board up to date, reviewing the handover procedure, etc.).

2. Identify all the people who will be involved with this change, including those who work both within and outside the unit.

3. Set up a small planning team and work through the change process.

4. Identify your feelings after you have worked through this change.

Further Reading

Douglas L M and Bevis E M (1979) *Nursing Management and Leadership in Action.* St Louis: C V Mosby.

Lancaster J and Lancaster W (1982) *Concepts for Advanced Nursing Practice: The Nurse as a Change Agent.* St Louis: C V Mosby.

Pearson A and Vaughan B (1984) Module 7. In: *A Systematic Approach to Nursing Care – An Introduction.* Milton Keynes: Open University.

16
Dilemmas in Practice

The purpose of this chapter is to:

- Raise an awareness of the moral dilemmas faced by nurses in everyday practice
- Give an outline of some ethical theories
- Discuss why different people may respond in different ways to moral dilemmas

For most people working in a service-orientated discipline such as nursing, moral dilemmas, that is, situations which necessitate a choice between alternatives which appear to be equally desirable or undesirable, always have and always will exist. While they have commonly given rise to discussion and debate it is only in more recent times that nurses have recognised their responsibility to make an active contribution in this arena. In the past, many mechanisms were established which effectively protected nurses from having formally to face moral dilemmas. The rigid bureaucratic structure with its strict system of rules, procedures and obedience left little room for participative nursing involvement. Furthermore, obedience to medical orders, a characteristic inherited from Florence Nightingale, has in fact protected nurses from having to take a stance on many moral issues.

While some people have laid the blame at the door of medicine, accusing doctors of acting as 'moral entrepreneurs' and claiming control over moral decision-making (Friedson, 1975), it could be argued that a contributing factor to the position they have taken has been the abdication by others of their responsibility. It is easy to say that a course of action was taken because it was ordered by another, even when there was concern about the appropriateness of the action and whether or not it complied with patients' wishes. But blind obedience to orders of this kind is no longer acceptable and, slowly but surely, nurses are recognising that they, too, have a contribution to make in moral decision-making.

As far back as 1953, the International Council of Nurses produced a code of ethics for nurses, most recently revised in 1974, in an attempt to offer some guidance about such a difficult subject. It was as recently as 1983, however, that British nurses first produced guidelines when the United Kingdom Council for Nursing, Midwifery and Health Visiting published a 'Code of Professional Conduct', revised a year later.

However, the production of such codes is fraught with difficulty. They cannot offer a 'textbook' answer to the many problems which are faced in day-to-day practice and, by the nature of the subject they cover, they are easily open to a variety of interpretations. For example, 'jeopardising safe standards of practice' (item No. 11) is dependent in the first instance on deciding what constitutes a safe standard. This in itself can vary from person to person since it is dependent on a belief in what constitutes good practice.

Thus, whilst the production of a code of professional conduct for nurses based on ethical principles is widely appreciated, it cannot be used as an alternative to developing an understanding of the process of moral decision-making and of the moral issues which nurses face. By the nature of the subject there are no right or wrong answers. However, some insight into the basis from which judgments are made can at least help to take away some of the confusion, hurt or even guilt which is often felt by people when faced with such situations.

CHOICE IN HEALTH CARE

It can be suggested that one of the reasons why we have become more aware of the moral dilemmas faced in health care today is the recognition of people's rights to some choice in how their health is managed. The days when the advice of medical practitioners was accepted without question are gone. Community Health Councils were established as a consequence of the 1974 reorganisation of the National Health Service, with a remit to represent the public. Likewise, there has been a steady increase in the number of consumer groups who put pressure on health care workers to provide access to information, to modify services and to include the 'consumer' in decision making. For example the work of the National Association for the Welfare of Children in Hospital (NAWCH) was instrumental in giving parents the right of open access to their children when in hospital.

More recently, there has been much debate about whether or not people should have access to their medical records. The media have also contributed to raising public awareness about rights and dilemmas through radio, film and television documentaries and plays, notably the play/film 'Whose Life is it, Anyway?' by Tom Stoppard, which gave rise to considerable debate.

It is not just the public whose stance is altering. There has also been a shift in emphasis of the value systems of nursing itself, with movement towards a school of thought known as humanistic existentialism. It has been suggested that within this philosophy '. . . are many of the ideas being discussed by nurses today such as the value of human beings, the quality of life and the freedom to choose – all topical subjects which are now widely debated by nurses' (Pearson and Vaughan, 1986).

While there has always been an option for patients to choose whether to accept or reject, obey or disobey, compliance within hospital care has traditionally been high. Indeed, patients have been unwilling to question or criticise since they see themselves as dependent and, sadly, it has been suggested that there is a fear of reprisal if they step out of line. Fortunately, many nurses now encourage patients to contribute to decisions about their own care, offering information, advice and guidance, but without pressure to comply if they do not wish to do so.

Inevitably, there are times when such situations can give rise to moral dilemmas. For instance, how does one respond when a patient is adamant that he does not wish to be moved during the night but the nurse is fearful that such a long period of immobility will lead to the development of pressure sores? How does one respond when treatment has been ordered by another professional carer which the patient refuses to accept? What is the answer when there are no beds available but the nurse is asked to accept a sick patient waiting in the Accident & Emergency Department? What can you do when a nurse is moved from your ward to another where the need may be even greater but, in your opinion, the levels of staff on your own ward have become unsafe? These are not necessarily world-shattering subjects which would give rise to wide public debate, as happens with euthanasia, abortion, genetic engineering or surrogacy; nevertheless, they are important and require immediate attention and a decision.

Nobody can give precise answers to such questions as these but, just like the people to whom we offer a service, we too have a choice in how we will respond and to some extent the way in which we behave is influenced by our ethical thinking. Yet if people who work together differ in their views of the way in which these problems should be handled, and it is almost inevitable that they will do so from time to time, there is potential for further conflict caused not only by the dilemma itself but also by the variance of opinion with a colleague over a sensitive issue.

ETHICAL THEORIES

Although many people use the words 'ethics' and 'morals' interchangeably, Campbell (1984) differentiates between the two. He suggests that '"ethics" is used to describe the formal study of morality, while "morals" is used to describe the particular actions, beliefs, attitudes and codes of rules which characterise different societies, groups and individuals'. Thus ethical theorists strive to describe different systems of morality in a non-judgmental way. A brief explanation of some theories which have been proposed can go some way to explaining why one person's judgments may vary from those of another at different times and in different situations.

Utilitarianism

This theory arises from the work of Jeremy Bentham (1748–1832) in the late eighteenth century, later expanded and modified by John Stuart Mill (1806–1873). Basically, it is concerned with the usefulness of decisions in providing happiness for as many people as possible and is sometimes described as the 'greatest good for the greatest number' theory.

In each case or situation an attempt is made to predict the outcomes of the actions and make a judgment about their influence. Thus, there is no absolute right or wrong but a balance is sought between the benefits and losses in each case and, at all times, the answer which is sought is the one which would provide the greatest good for the greatest number.

While at first sight this may seem to be quite straightforward, it is, of course, fraught with difficulties, the most obvious being who should be the judge of the greatest good. Bentham was unconcerned with the quality of goodness or happiness, suggesting that each person's quota should be of equal importance. This view was modifed by Mill who brought in the notion of quality, happiness of the mind being, in his opinion, of the highest order. But the question of who should judge happiness still remains. In Campbell's (1984b) words, 'Here Mill appealed to the competent judge. Only the person who knows both "higher" and "lower" pleasures is competent to judge between them. Thus Socrates is a better judge of happiness than a fool'. There are many who would challenge an assumption of this nature.

Campbell suggests that utilitarian theory was the influential drive behind many of the social reforms of the nineteenth century, such as public provision of health, the enhanced status of women and improved conditions of employment. A further extension of this can be seen with the introduction of the National Health Service in 1948. Yet even such an apparently altruistic act is beset with difficulties since it gives rise to all sorts of problems in the provision of sufficient resources to meet the needs of all the people. This can be seen at a level nearer home when one starts wondering about the extra patient waiting in the Accident & Emergency Department. Which is the better solution, to spread the resources so thinly that everyone gets a little or to maintain an agreed standard of service for a lesser number of people but deprive the person who is waiting?

In the same way, it raises questions about the provision of services. Which will provide greater good, an improvement in services to the elderly whose life expectancy is limited, or greater investment in the management of premature infants who potentially have a long and fruitful life ahead of them? Unpleasant as choices of this kind are, someone has to make judgments since there is no bottomless purse of money for health care.

Of course, there can be no right or wrong answers to these questions, merely opinions expressed by different people but, from a utilitarian viewpoint, it can be argued that a greater number would suffer if one more patient was admitted and standards could not be maintained. Yet this gives rise to serious concern about the way in which minority groups would fare. The man waiting in the Accident & Emergency Department could be seen to represent a minority group, and caring for his well-being might jeopardise the services to all the other patients. But can his needs be ignored?

A further issue to note is that the consequences or outcomes of an act cannot always be predicted accurately and, if they are not as expected, how can they be justified? It may seem unfair, yet we all know that there have been times when we have made the decision to take a risk and 'got away with it', while someone who has apparently followed all the rules has ended in an unsatisfactory situation. Yet whose behaviour was morally acceptable?

Duty

Another school of thought is that propounded by Emmanuel Kant (1742–1804) which is concerned with duty and more formally known as deontology. Those who take this stance believe that it is possible to make 'absolute' statements which should be followed at all times, the most obvious being the rule to preserve life. They are not concerned with what is good or bad, as in the utilitarian approach, but with what is right or wrong. Thus, rules or principles become the basis of morality. Actions which conform to the principles are all-important, regardless of the outcomes.

Such a stance obviously has a very strong influence on the way in which health care is offered. In Kant's view, it was possible to identify universal principles of duty which would stand the test of time and apply in all circumstances. Actions would then be determined by duties, regardless of the outcomes. Telling the truth may be a clear example here. According to this moral code truth-telling must be adhered to at all times yet, as we all know, there are times when this presents difficulties. Do you tell a friend that you really dislike something he has just bought at great expense leaving him hurt and offended? Or do you adjust your words, or just keep quiet? In the same way, it may be considered a duty that all patients should be told their diagnosis and prognosis under any circumstances. What of those who do not wish to receive such information?

Another issue which raises questions in relation to duty is that of patients' obligations to behave in such a way as to minimise risks to their health. There has been a growing interest in the concept of self-care, that is a 'process whereby a lay person functions on his/her own behalf in health promotion and prevention, and in disease detection and treatment' (Levin et al, 1979). Does this mean that those who choose not to fulfil their obligations or duties, by either omission or inappropriate action are not fulfilling their moral role? If this is so, should they then be denied the right of access to health care? For example, is it morally acceptable to deny someone medical or nursing services because he or she continues to smoke, takes no exercise or does not lose weight? What happens, then, to our duty as nurses to offer an unconditional, non-judgmental service to patients? There are some health-care workers who feel that withholding services under these sorts of conditions is justifiable behaviour and that the notion that people should not harm themselves must be met.

Thus, while patient autonomy, that is the freedom to make one's own decisions about oneself, may be upheld in a deontological approach, patients' rights to an unconditional service may not always follow. If patients fail to comply with their own duty to behave in such a way as to maximise good health, does this negate the health-care worker's duty to provide a service. Furthermore, how far can such a principle be taken? What about the elderly patient with a venous ulcer who fails to keep a pressure bandage on her leg. Should the service to dress the ulcer be withdrawn because of a failure of duty in following recommended treatment. The implications of such a line of thought would be unacceptable to many nurses yet the principle of duty is often used at a different level in day-to-day practice.

Rights

Rights theory is basically concerned with a respect for people and, most importantly, their freedom to choose. It implies a respect of others and, in Campbell's (1984b) words, 'Respect . . . implies a relationship of involvement with other persons, such that our choices and intentions are governed by their aims and aspirations as well as our own'.

The implications of rights theory are that a person's rights must be respected regardless of the outcomes. Thus if someone refuses treatment, even if it is known that the outcome may give rise to serious consequences, his or her decision must be respected. The most obvious example is the right of the Jehovah's Witness to refuse a blood transfusion even though this may result in his or her death. A more common example is the one given earlier of someone refusing to be moved even though this may give rise to the risk of forming pressure sores. In the same way the right to continued treatment of the leg ulcer would be respected.

A further consideration is how much freedom of action one has when the actions may be harmful to others. Is it a human right to choose to continue to smoke in an enclosed environment such as an office space where others may be harmed by passive smoking? Can one choose to play loud music late at night which may annoy a neighbour? Have all people the right to hospital admission, even though this may jeopardise the standards of care offered to other patients? Think back to the man waiting in the Accident & Emergency Department for a bed; has he the right to admission even though everyone else would be put at risk by lowering the standards below a safe level? There is no simple or right answer to questions such as these but it can be seen that following a different moral code would lead to different outcomes.

Rights theory strongly emphasises patient autonomy and, alongside this, the right to have access to information and to know all the risks. But the question, 'What constitutes a risk?' has then to be asked. If, for example, there is a very small risk, say, less than 1 in 1000 chance, of a patient experiencing an adverse side effect from treatment, should that information be given to him before consent is gained?

Risk-taking is part of everyday life yet it is unlikely that we consciously think about it all the time. Indeed, if we looked at all the risk we do take in such things as crossing the road or driving a car, our lives would become intolerable. It is in the unusual situations, such as having an anaesthetic, where people may not know of the risk of possible side effects, that the question is more difficult to answer. How much information do they have a right to before being reasonably asked to give consent?

A further question for debate following the rights school of thought is the point at which rights are relinquished. The laws of our society set down some limits to rights, as is evidenced by the control which is exerted over people deemed to be psychiatrically disabled. If people break the law by stealing or harming others their right to freedom is relinquished. Thus it can be seen that society links rights with responsibility and once responsibility is acknowledged there is also an obligation to answer or account for one's actions.

There are instances where responsibility can be excused, through, for example, unavoidable ignorance, and this can be linked back to allocation of work. It can be suggested that a manager has a responsibility to ensure that an individual is capable of the work he or she is asked to do. If work is given to someone and it is beyond her capacity to recognise that she does not have the skill to fulfil it, that person cannot reasonably be held responsible for any inclement outcome. Similarly, some circumstances can mitigate responsibility, as when, for example, very low staffing levels mean that it is impossible to provide sufficient supervision of a patient, who consequently comes to some harm; provided that attempts have been made to try to correct the situation, responsibilities would have been fulfilled and the person's rights would be protected.

CLINICAL DILEMMAS

The sort of moral dilemmas which are talked about openly, such as euthanasia or abortion, are not necessarily those which give rise to concern in everyday practice. It is often the small things which play on one's mind over a period of time, causing a continuing worry. For nurses there are three broad areas which we meet regularly and have to make decisions about in everyday practice: consent, truth-telling and confidentiality.

Consent

Informed consent has become an accepted part of practice in health care today, although the degree to which it is practised is still questionable. However, it is worth noting that in America much of the law is based on rights theory, that is the right to know the risk of action or non-action; thus, informed consent has become central to practice.

At first sight, this may seem to be highly commendable but, like most things, it has brought problems with it, leading to an approach to practice which is 'litigation conscious' and has been called defensive practice. The fear of being sued for malpractice has led to great caution by practitioners who may, as a consequence, be unwilling to accept 'difficult' cases or to be creative in their approach. In turn, this has meant that some people have difficulty in finding a practitioner willing to offer them treatment. It can be suggested that exercising rights to this extent, that is to the level where every risk, however small, must be made explicit before consent is gained, has had a detrimental effect on the service which is available to people.

In reality, most people take a utilitarian approach to consent, giving information about major risks or side effects but not all possible eventualities and, on consideration, this is how most of us live our lives. We know there is some risk in flying but few people know the actual 'odds', or details of what could go wrong. Yet the majority accept these risks and still go on flying; in other words, we consent without full knowledge.

Maybe the most important thing to remember is that there are those people who wish to have access to more detail than is usual about what will or may happen to them and, surely, it is both their right and our duty to provide such information if required.

Truth-Telling

'How much to tell' is another problem which nurses often face. We have come from a tradition where it was the province of doctors to decide when and what to tell patients. But, in practice, it is usually nurses who spend most time with patients and they are often the ones who can form the closest relationships, especially in difficult times. As we all know, living with a secret is an uncomfortable state to be in, especially when a moral obligation to tell the truth is felt. It can lead to distancing, avoidance and poor communication, all of which can be detrimental to patient care.

Open discussion amongst a multidisciplinary team of health workers can often overcome some of these difficulties, since the most common cause is lack of awareness of the awkwardness which can be created. Once the problems have been confronted and openly discussed they can usually be resolved. Having said that, it must also be said that there is a right *not* to know as well as the right to know. While there may be a strong belief in sharing information with patients, sensitivity to those who do not wish for more knowledge must surely be respected.

Confidentiality

What do you do if a colleague reveals to you in confidence that she is taking drugs. Or a patient tells you, again in confidence, that his injuries were inflicted by another person? Again, there is a conflict between duty and respect of persons. Probably the simplest way of dealing with this sort of situation is to avoid it ever happening in the first place. To give an absolute promise of silence can leave you in a very difficult situation whereas a tentative suggestion that you must be left some room to make a judgment does not usually hamper the discussion.

At the end of the day, it is usually the utilitarian approach which wins, that is consideration of the outcomes of revealing or not revealing the information which has been imparted. There are, of course, some situations where the law of the land will require that confidential information is divulged, but it is always wise to seek guidance if such circumstances arise.

The purpose behind this chapter has not been to try to give answers to the way in which one can handle moral dilemmas. In the last instance, no-one can tell you what is right or wrong, good or bad, and the way you behave must be between you and your conscience. Yet some insight, however brief, into different schools of thought related to ethical theory may at least help in understanding some of the reasoning behind moral decision-making and why different people respond in different ways.

Unfortunately, there is never a simple answer to the questions which are asked and there will always be uncertainty in this complex area. Indeed, it would be arrogant to think that anyone knew the answers all the time. But the issues which are raised cannot be ignored and surely it is better and easier to face them with some understanding than to deny their very existence?

EXERCISES

1. Write down at least two incidents in which you have been involved recently which have entailed making a moral judgment.

2. Do you think your decision was influenced by any of the schools of thought outlined above, namely:

- By consideration of outcomes?
- By reason of duty?
- By human rights?

If so, how did they influence your actions? Were there others involved who held the same, or different, views as you did? Have you had an opportunity to talk to them, especially if there was a difference of opinion?

3. Do you include discussion of moral dilemmas during ward report/meetings? Maybe this could be an agenda item on one of these occasions?

Further Reading

Campbell A (1984) *Moral Dilemmas in Medicine*. Edinburgh: Churchill Livingstone.

Tschudin V (1986) *Ethics in Nursing: The Caring Relationship*. London: Heinemann Nursing.

References

Armitage P (1983) Joint working in primary health care. Occasional paper. *Nursing Times*, **79**: 75–78.

Athlone (1938) *Interim Report of the Inter-Departmental Committee on Nursing Services*. London: HMSO.

Benner P (1984) *From Novice to Expert: Excellence and Power in Clinical Nursing Practice*. Reading, MA: Addison-Wesley.

Bennis W G (1970) Beyond bureaucracy. In: *American Bureaucracy*, ed. Bennis W G. Chicago: Aldmie.

Bevis E M (1978) *Curriculum Building in Nursing: A Process*. St Louis: C V Mosby.

Bloch D (1977) Criteria, standards and norms. *Journal of Advanced Nursing Administration*, September, 20–30.

Bond J and Bond S (1986) *Sociology and Health Care. An Introduction for Nurses and other Health Care Professionals*. Edinburgh: Churchill Livingstone.

Brown W and Jacques E (1965) *Glacier Project Papers*. London: Heinemann.

Burnard P (1985) *Learning Human Skills*. London: Heinemann.

Burnip S (1987) *Ward Profiles*. Unpublished report, Oxford Health Authority.

Bush H A (1979) Models for nursing. *Advances in Nursing*, **1**(2): 13–21.

Calnan M (1987) *Health and Illness – The Lay Perspective*. London: Tavistock Publications.

Campbell A (1984a) *Moderated Love. A Theology of Professional Care*. London: SPCK

Campbell A (1984b) *Moral Dilemmas in Medicine*. Edinburgh: Churchill Livingstone.

Causier P (1982) What's in store – a nurse for equipment. *Nursing Times*, **78**(29): 1225–1227.

Claus K and Bailey J (1977) *Power and Influence in Health Care. A New Approach to Leadership*. St Louis: C V Mosby.

Cormack D (ed.) (1984) *The Research Process in Nursing*. Oxford: Blackwell Scientific Publications.

Cox T (1978) *Stress*. London: Macmillan.

Cunningham A. (1980) *Staff Nurses and their Reasons for Leaving*. Unpublished thesis, Edinburgh University.

Data Protection Act. (1986) London: HMSO.

Davies C (1976) Experience of dependency and control in work: the case of nurses. *Journal of Advanced Nursing*, **1**(4): 273–282.

Davies I K (1976) *Objectives in Curriculum Design*. Maidenhead: McGraw-Hill.

DHSS (1969) *Report of the Working Party on Management Structure in Local Authority Nursing Services (Mayston Report)*. London: HMSO.

DHSS (1972) *Report of the Committee on Nursing (Briggs Report)*. London: HMSO.

DHSS (1982) *Communication and Care Package*. London: HMSO.

DHSS (1983) *NHS Management Inquiry (Griffiths Report)*. London: HMSO.

DHSS (1984) *Nurse Manpower Project*

for NHS Management Inquiry. A Comparison of Some Methods of Estimating the Requirement for Nursing Staff. London: HMSO.

DHSS (1986) Mix and Match. A Review of Nursing Skills. London: HMSO.

DHSS (1986) Neighbourhood Nursing: A Focus for Care. A Report of the Community Nursing Review (Cumberlege Report). London: HMSO.

DHSS & SHHD (1966) Report of the Committee on Senior Nursing Staff Structure (Salmon Report). London: HMSO.

Dewey J (1961) Democracy and Education. New York: The Free Press.

Dickson A (1982) A Woman in Her Own Right. Assertiveness and You. London: Quartet Books.

Dingwall R (1980) Problems in teamwork in primary care. In: Teamwork in the Personal Social Services and Health Care, eds. Lonsdale S, Webb A, and Briggs T L, pp. 111–137. London: Croom Helm.

Donald J G (1976) Contracting for Learning. Learning Development 2.

Donnelly D F (1978) The assertive nurse. Nursing, 78(8): 65–69.

Douglas L M and Bevis E M (1979) Nursing Management and Leadership in Action. St Louis: C V Mosby.

Elhart D (1978) Scientific Principles in Nursing. St Louis: C V Mosby.

Faulkner A (1980) Communication and the nurse. Nursing Times, 76(36): Suppl 21, 93–95.

Fawcett J (1978) The 'What' of Theory Development. Is Theory Theory Development? What how? New York National League for Nurses.

Fielder F E (1967) A Theory of Leadership Effectiveness. New York: McGraw-Hill.

Friedson E (1975) Profession of Medicine. New York: Dodd, Mead and Co.

Galassi J, Galassi M and Vedder M (1981) Perspectives on

assertiveness as a social skills model. In: Social Competence, eds. Wine J and Smye H. New York: Guildford Press.

Goldstone L, Ball J A and Collier M M (1983) Monitor: An Index of the Quality of Nursing Care for Acute Medical and Surgical Wards. Newcastle upon Tyne: Polytechnic Productions Ltd.

Goode W J (1969) The theoretical limits of professionalisation. In: The Semi-Professions and Their Organization, Etzioni A, pp. 266–313. New York: The Free Press.

Hare R H (1964) Adolescents in adults. In: Aims in Education, ed. Hollins T H B. Manchester: Manchester University Press.

Hawthorne P (1983) Principles of research – checklist. Nursing Times, 79(35): 41–43.

Hayward J (1975) Information: A Prescription Against Pain. RCN Research Series. London: Royal College of Nursing.

Health Education Council (1987) That's the Limit. London: Health Education Council.

Herzberg F (1959) The Motivation to Work. New York: John Wiley and Sons.

Hingley P and Harris P (1986) Burnout at senior level. Nursing Times, 82(31): 28–29.

Holmes T H and Rahe R H (1967) The social adjustment rating scale. Journal of Psychosomatic Research, 11: 213–218.

International Council of Nurses (1965) The International Code of Ethics for Nurses. Geneva: International Council of Nurses.

Iwasin C L (1987) The role of the teacher in self-directed learning. Nurse Education Today, 7: 222–227.

Jacobi E M (1976) The Status of Continuing Education Programmes for Nurses in the United States. London: King Edward's Hospital Fund.

Jarvis P (1983) Professional Education. London: Croom Helm.

Jarvis P (1985) *The Sociology of Adult and Continuing Education*. London: Croom Helm.

Kelley D and Connor D R (1979) The emotional cycle of change. In: *The Annual Handbook for Group Facilitators*, Jones J E and Pfeiffer J W. La Jolla, CA: University Associates.

Keyser D (1986) Using nursing contracts to support change in nursing organisations. *Nurse Education Today*, **6**: 103–108.

King I M (1981) *A Theory of Nursing: Systems, Concepts, Process*. New York: John Wiley and Sons.

Kinston W (1987) *Stronger Nursing Organisation*. Brunel Institute of Organisation and Social Structure.

Kitson A L (1986) Indicators of quality in nursing care – an alternative aproach. *Journal of Advanced Nursing*, **11**(2): 133–144.

Knowles M (1978) *The Adult Learner: A Neglected Species*. Houston: Gulf Publishing Co.

Knowles M (1980) *The Modern Practice of Adult Education*. Chicago: Association Press.

Lancaster J and Lancaster W (1982) *Concepts for Advanced Nursing Practice – The Nurse as a Change Agent*. St Louis: C V Mosby.

Levin L (1979) *Self-care: Lay Initiatives in Health*. New York: Prodist.

Lewin K (1951) *Field Theory in Social Science*. New York: Harper and Row.

Lewis F M and Batey M V (1982) Clarifying autonomy and accountability in nursing services, part 2. *Journal of Nursing Administration*, **12**(10): 10–15.

Lippitt G L (1973) *Visualising Change: Model Guidelines and the Change Process*. La Jolla, CA: University Associates.

Lupton T (1971) *Management and the Social Sciences*. Harmondsworth: Penguin.

Macleod Clark J (1983) Nurse–patient communication. In: *Nursing Research: Ten Studies in Patient Care*, ed. Wilson-Barnett J. Chichester: John Wiley and Sons.

McGregor D (1960) *The Human Side of Enterprise*. New York: McGraw-Hill.

McGuisley J (1900) A case for rehousing upstream: the political economy of illness. In: *Patients, Physicians and Illness. A sourcebook in behavioural science and health*, ed. Jaco E G. New York: Free Press.

Manthey M (1978) *The Practice of Primary Nursing*. Oxford: Blackwell Scientific Publications.

Maslach C (1982) *Burn Out: The Cost of Care*. New Jersey: Prentice-Hall.

Maslow A H (1954) *Motivation and Personality*, 2nd edn. 1970. New York: Harper and Row.

Menzies I E P (1960) *A Case Study in the Functioning of Social Systems as a Defence Against Anxiety*. London: Tavistock Institute of Human Relations.

Ministry of Health (1966) *Report of the Committee on Senior Staff Structure (Schuman Report)*. London: HMSO.

Moores B (1987) The changing composition of the British hospital nursing workforce. *Journal of Advanced Nursing*, **12**(4): 499–504.

Neuman B (1982) *The Neuman Systems Model*. East Norwalk, CT: Appleton-Century-Crofts.

Nightingale F (1859) *Notes on Nursing: What It Is and What It Is Not*. London: Harrison (reprinted by J B Lippincott in 1946).

Olson J and Kartha A (1983) *Use of Self-directed Learning in Post-RN Education*. Proceedings of a Conference on Graduate Education. Vancouver: University of British Columbia.

Orem D E (1980) *Nursing Concepts of Practice*. New York: McGraw-Hill.

Pearson A (1983) *The Clinical Nursing Unit*. London: Heinemann.

Pearson A (1987) *Living in a Plaster Cast – How Nursing Can Help*.

RCN Research Series. London: Royal College of Nursing.

Pearson A (ed) (1987) *Primary Nursing – Nursing in the Burford and Oxford Nursing Development Units.* London: Croom Helm.

Pearson A (ed) (1987) *Nursing Quality Measurement – Quality Assurance Methods for Peer Review.* Chichester: HM+M/John Wiley and Sons.

Pearson A and Vaughan B (1984) Module 7. In: *A Systematic Approach to Nursing Care – An Introduction.* Milton Keynes: Open University.

Pearson A and Vaughan B (1986) *Models for Nursing Practice.* London: Heinemann.

Pembrey S (1980) *The Ward Sister – Key to Nursing.* RCN Research Series. London; Royal College of Nursing.

Peplau H E (1952) *Interpersonal Relationships in Nursing.* New York: Putnam Publishing Group.

Peters R S (1966) *Ethics and Education.* London: Allen and Unwin.

Phelps S and Ansal (1975) *The Assertive Woman.* San Luis Obispo, CA: Impact Publishers.

Philp T (1983) *Making Performance Appraisal Work.* Maidenhead: McGraw-Hill.

Pietroni P (1986) *The Healing Arts.* Television Broadcast.

Puetz B (1985) *Evaluation in Nursing Staff Development: Method and Models.* Rockville, MD: Aspen Systems Corporation.

RCN (1943) *Report of Education and Training Committee (Chairman: Lord Horder).* London: Royal College of Nursing.

RCN (1964) *A Reform of Nurse Education (Platt Report).* London: Royal College of Nursing.

RCN (1978) *The Report of the Working Party on Counselling.* London: Royal College of Nursing.

RCN (1985) *The Report on the Commission on Nurse Education.* London: Royal College of Nursing.

RCN (1987) *How to Find Information.* London: Royal College of Nursing.

RCN Association of Nursing Education (1987) *Performance Indicators in Nurse Education.* London: Royal College of Nursing.

Reedy B L E C (1980) Teamwork in primary health care: a conspectus. In: *Primary Care,* ed. pp. 108–138. London: Heinemann.

Romano J and Bellack A (1980) Social assertive behaviour. *Journal of Consulting & Clinical Psychology.*

Roper N, Logan W and Tierney A (1985) *The Elements of Nursing.* Edinburgh: Churchill Livingstone.

Roy C (1976) *Introduction to Nursing: An Adaptation Model.* Englewood Cliffs, NJ: Prentice-Hall.

Schein E (1969) The mechanisms of change. In: *Planning Change,* Bennis W G. New York: Holt, Reinhart and Winston.

Schwartz G E (1975) Biofeedback. Self-regulation and the patterning of physiological processes. *American Scientist,* **63**: 314–324.

Scottish Home and Health Department (1969) *Nursing Workload as a Basis for Staffing – Report of the Work Study Department of the North East Regional Hospital Board, Scotland.* Scottish Health Services Studies No. 9 (Aberdeen Formula) SHAD. Edinburgh: HMSO.

Simpson I H (1979) *From Student to Nurse – A Longitudinal Study of Socialisation.* New York: Cambridge University Press.

Smith M (1975) *When I Say No I Feel Guilty.* New York: Bantam Books.

Stewart V and Stewart A (1981) *Managing the Poor Performer.* Aldershot: Gower Publishing.

Stilwell B (1982) The nurse

practitioner at work. *Nursing Times*, **78**: 1779–1803.

Styles M (1982) *On Nursing: Towards a New Endowment*. St Louis: C V Mosby.

Taylor F W (1947) *Scientific Management*. New York: Harper and Row.

Telford W A (1979) *Determining Nursing Establishments*. Birmingham: East Birmingham Health Authority.

Tietjen T (1978) *How Am I Doing?* Watford: Video Arts Ltd.

Torrance C (1983) *Pressure Sores – Aetiology, Treatment and Prevention*. London: Croom Helm.

Treece E W and Treece J W (1975) *Elements of Research in Nursing*. St Louis: C V Mosby.

Tschudin V (1985) Too much pressure. *Nursing Times*, **81**: 30–31.

UKCC (1984) *Code of Professional Conduct for the Nurse, Midwife and Health Visitor*. London: UKCC.

UKCC (1986) *Project 2000. A New Preparation for Practice*. London: UKCC.

UKCC (1987) *Mandatory Periodic Refreshment for Nurses and Health Visitors*. Discussion Paper. London: UKCC.

Ullrich R A and Wieland G P (1980) *Organisational Theory and Design*. Homerod, Ill: Richard D Irwin Inc.

Vaughan B (1986) *Preparing a Ward Philosophy*. Unpublished paper, Oxford Health Authority.

Vaughan B (1987) Discharge from hospital following surgery. *Nursing Times*, **84**: 28–31.

Wandelt M and Ager J (1974) *Quality Patients Care Scale*. East Norwalk, CT: Appleton-Century-Crofts.

Wilson-Barnett J and Fordham M (1982) *Recovery from Illness*. Chichester: John Wiley and Sons.

Wright S (1987) Consuming interests. *Senior Nurse*, **6**(2): 24–26.

Index

systems   214
motivation   38
motivator factors   39–40

National Association for the Welfare
   of Children in Hospital
   (NAWCH)   212
National Childbirth Trust   4
National Health Service   69, 212, 215
national policy   177
noise   70
norms   99–101
nurse education   109
   see also professional education
nurse practitioner   54, 109–10, 113
nurses' role   4, 54
nursing actions   8, 10, 19, 49, 101,
   120, 128, 151
nursing analysis and evaluation
   20–1, 166–70
nursing assessment   6, 72, 100, 165,
   207
nursing behaviours   86–8
nursing care conferences   152
nursing function   5, 8, 11
nursing methods   50–1, 85
   see also nursing process
nursing models   37, 90, 164–6, 179
nursing practice   10, 12, 15, 84, 127,
   163
nursing prescription   19, 54, 61, 96,
   100, 177
   implementation of   166
nursing problems   47, 152
nursing process   3, 29, 47–8, 56, 114,
   165–6
   description of   16–21
   evaluation of   168–9
   and patient involvement   24
   and stress   136
nursing records   168–9
nursing review   19
nursing service   9, 24, 37, 166, 170,
   174, 216
   quality of   21, 163
   and standards of care   161–2, 166
   and stress   135
nursing standards   48–9, 170–1 (Fig
   12.4)
nursing structures   15, 26–7, 173–4,
   184
nursing team   76, 83, 85–6, 92

nursing work   29, 49, 59, 148, 199,
   205

objectives   3, 39, 166, 206, 209
   learning   114
   see also goals
occupational therapist   9, 148, 183
orientation programme   102

partnership   24–5
patient/client allocation   53, 60–1,
   152, 155
patient outcomes   151, 170
performance appraisal   95
   see also staff appraisal
performance review   34, 90, 95–107,
   115, 149, 162
   communication and   68
   and quality assurance   22
performance standards   98–102, 104
   document   98–102
permissive leadership   41–2
personalised care/service   29, 34–5,
   38, 47–9, 51, 53, 57, 206–7
personality traits   41, 58, 185, 205
   'Type A/Type B'   133
personal space   189, 193
personnel services   177–8
philosophy   56, 83–7
   educational   109
   of nursing care   15–21, 76, 83–7,
      164, 213
   of unit   81, 84
pilot study   123, 125
planning   36–7, 46, 151, 157–8, 167,
   209
   care   83, 155, 161, 207
   career   105
   for discharge   34, 149
   forward   149
positive trigger   69
posture   188–9
power   10, 41, 73, 186, 199
   in health care   7–8
   lack of   200
   legitimate   25
   sources/distribution of   7, 26–7, 48,
      205, 208–9
praise   185, 194–5
precarious stability   86–7
primary nurse   53–5, 97, 104, 176–7,
   182
   and accountability   61